# QUEEN OF THE
# SEVEN CROSSROADS

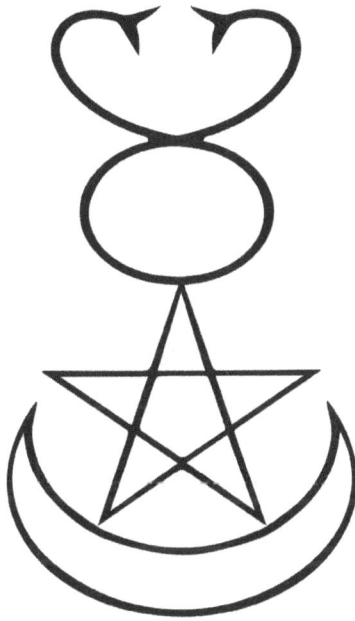

## HUMBERTO MAGGI

ISBN 978-1-907881-87-9 (Hardcover)
ISBN 978-1-907881-88-6 (Paperback)

A catalogue for this title is available from the British Library.
10 9 8 7 6 5 4 3 2 1

First published in 2020 by Hadean Press
West Yorkshire
England

WWW.HADEANPRESS.COM

# Queen of the
# Seven Crossroads

Humberto Maggi

# CONTENTS

# INTRODUCTION

———— •◆• ————

The Queens of Quimbanda, Queens of Magic and Sorcery, and Queens of Hell are considered to be powerful spirits who deserve great honors and reverence. To each of them are assigned Astral Kingdoms that govern over different aspects of magical work and that connect with the mundane plane strongly at specific places and times, though their power in truth knows no limits or boundaries.

Like the dead heroines of older times, who received cult and were expected to aid the living, the Queens of Quimbanda, as with most of the lesser spirits in this system, are reputed to have been extraordinary whilst living – for good or evil. The diabolical aesthetics and the historical origins of Quimbanda associated and associate these women with the Devil – although here the Devil is not seen as the orthodoxies teach. Quimbanda moves toward a restoration of the original cosmogonies misrepresented by the Christian churches. It accepts the superficial ideas and images developed by Christianity to accuse and to frighten, but proposes a core interpretation that in the end completely undermines Christian theologies.

The Quimbanda that arose in Brazil is a fig tree with roots in European witchcraft and African religions; it is the inheritance of people who were exiled and enslaved – at its core it is reaction and rebellion against Church and State, against Inquisition and Slavery.

History and myth come together to create and continuously develop the definitions and the interpretations of who or what the Queens of Quimbanda are. Research and revelation compose this short treatise dedicated to the Queen of the Seven Crossroads with whom I have being working for several years. She came into my life at a moment of great and difficult change, and she has guided me faithfully since then. Often experiences with the Queen of the Seven Crossroads are frightful – but there is always a surreptitious feeling that things are under control and all is for the best. These are entities that test and improve their protégées.

The idea of writing a short treatise on the Queen of the Seven Crossroads came to me during one of the works I do regularly with her. I have a large image of her at home, and a smaller one that travels with me wherever I go. Under her guidance we are going to survey the historical developments that influenced the creation of this concept in the Quimbanda that emerged in the first half of the 20th century in Brazil, as well as the ideas and techniques inherited both from Europe and Africa; we also are going to follow the thread of inspirations I received and we will borrow from the practices I learned both as a Chief of Quimbanda and as a researcher.

The aim of this treatise is then to provide the conceptual background for a better comprehension of the identity and role of the Queen of the Seven Crossroads which will enable the devotee to develop a consistent practice of work and communion with this elevated spirit.

*Humberto Maggi*

# THE QUEENS OF MAGIC

————— ◆ —————

The most preeminent female spirit in Quimbanda is Maria Padilha, a spirit inspired by the wife of King Peter of Castile. She is usually considered the main source for the creation of the concept of the "queen" in Quimbanda. Around her a legend of beauty, cruelty and deceit was developed – although the historical character of Maria de Padilla (1334-1361) in truth left behind memories of being a good-hearted and pious woman. Her close relationships with the Jews in the court of King Peter, and the association of them with magic, helped to create the legendary connection between Maria de Padilla and sorcery that blossomed in the later *Romancero* and in the witchcraft spells.

The *Romancero* is a collection of folk ballads that appeared around the late 14th and early 15th centuries and which inherited themes, influences and inspirations from the epic tradition, and from the literature that developed around the Arthurian or Charlemagne legends.[1] In the *Romancero*, Maria de Padilla is often pictured as an evil seductress with connections to magic, which associates her with previous figures renowned for their dangerous beauty and magical powers: Circe, Medea, and Morgana.

---

1 "Romancero." Encyclopædia Britannica, 13 Jan. 2015, www. britannica.com/art/romancero.

# Circe

We meet Circe for the first time when Odysseus arrives at her island in chapter ten of the *Odyssey*; the "isle of Aeaea, where dwelt fair-tressed Circe, a dread goddess of human speech"[2] reveals itself to be a dreadful place of danger for the hero and his companions. Circe is the daughter of the god Helius ("who gives light to mortals") and she is found in a house built of polished stone, guarded by mountain wolves and lions bewitched by "evil drugs". The animals were very friendly towards the visitors, and Circe herself acted as a kind host: she bade them in, seated them, and offered "a portion of cheese and barley meal and yellow honey with Pramnian wine". But it was all a trap:

> [...] but in the food she mixed baneful drugs, that they might utterly forget their native land. Now when she had given them the potion, and they had drunk it off, then she presently smote them with her wand, and penned them in the sties. And they had the heads, and voice, and bristles, and shape of swine, but their minds remained unchanged even as before.[3]

Circe operated her evil and baneful magic with drugs and a magical wand, a ῥάβδῳ (*rabdo*). She is not the only one in the *Odyssey* who uses a wand to perform magic, however. In chapter thirteen, the goddess Athena turns the god-like Odysseus into a decrepit beggar just by touching him with her ῥάβδῳ. The power of transformation seems to rely on the wands, as the effect of the drugs is described as causing the men forget their home.

---

2 Homer, and A. T. Murray. *The Odyssey, with an English Translation*. W. Heinemann, 1938.

3 Od. 10.235-240.

Queen of the Seven Crossroads

In the final chapter of the *Odyssey* another god appears waving a ῥάβδῳ: Hermes. Hermes' ῥάβδῳ however displays a different set of powers:

Meanwhile Cyllenian Hermes called forth the spirits of the wooers. He held in his hands his wand, a fair wand of gold, wherewith he lulls to sleep the eyes of whom he will, while others again he wakens even out of slumber; with this he roused and led the spirits, and they followed gibbering.[4]

Hermes' ῥάβδῳ has power over sleep and *over the souls of the dead*. This is very interesting for us because the iconography of Quimbanda depicts the Queen of the Seven Crossroads as bearing a wand with a white skull at the top. The white skull in Quimbanda is generally associated with the souls of the dead. But the golden wand of Hermes, given to him by his brother Apollo, also possessed the faculty of uniting in love all beings divided by hate – love and love unions are one of the traditional areas of activity of the feminine spirits of Quimbanda.

The connection of Hermes with the crossroads also indicates to us the ancient tradition that survives in the title of the Queen; more than that, the rulership of Hermes over streets, roads and the market square brings him very close to the African deity Eshu who has similar attributions. Here European and African roads of tradition start to meet at the crossroads of Quimbanda: the Queen of the Seven Crossroads is a *pombagira* or *female-exu*. The exus of Quimbanda were created after the model of the orishá Eshu, as we will soon see. Like Hermes, Eshu is also a trickster and a magician, and a deity intimately associated with the crossroads:

---

4 Od. 24.1-10.

The crossroads is a major concept in African religion. It is a pervasive idea that suggests there is a point where good and evil, humanity and divinity, the living and the Dead, the night and the day, and all other contradictions, opposites, and situations involving decisions must meet. At this point, there exists an intermediary to open the way, to provide humans with choice, and to teach wisdom at the gate. This gatekeeper goes by many names, but is known in the Yoruba as Legba, Eshu, or Ellegua depending on the language and country of practice.[5]

Medea draining the blood of Aeson in order to rejuvenate him with her special brew. Engraving. Credit: Wellcome Collection. Attribution 4.0 International (CC BY 4.0)

---

5 Asante, Molefi Kete., et al. *Encyclopedia of African Religion.* SAGE, 2009.

# Medea

Medea was the niece of Circe and reputed to be a priestess of Hecate. The two main sources about her are the *Argonautica* of Apollonius of Rhodes and the tragedy by her name written by Euripides. She shared with her aunt divine descent and some sources believed she attained some kind of immortality and received cult honors – a true and accomplished heroine.

But even more than Circe, Medea inspired horror, due to the killing of her own children to avenge herself for her betrayal and abandonment by Jason. Seduced with the aid of Aphrodite, Medea had betrayed father and country for her lover, deserting her homeland and killing a brother in the process. Later, when Jason decided to leave her to marry a rich princess and force her into exile, she avenged herself by killing the bride, the father of the bride, and the two sons she had with Jason.[6] She is very well described in the following words:

> A vivid portrait of a woman empowered by her exclusion from society, alive with passion and the suffering of wounded love.[7]

The myth of Medea narrates a story that could be perfectly applied to a *pombagira*; the narratives we find in Quimbanda about the former lives of these spirits are full of tragic situations like these. Many of stories are about the *pombagiras* who suffered treason and persecution but who also committed horrible deeds.

Medea was an accomplished sorceress. Painted scenes in *hydriai* depicted Medea working her rejuvenating magic in large

---

6 Although there are variations of the myth where she is not the killer of her children, the death of the children is a common element of most of the different narratives.

7 Griffiths, Emma. *Medea*. Routledge, 2006.

cauldrons placed over blazing fires, one of the earliest examples of the popular motif of the witch with her cauldron. In the *Argonautica* by Apollonius Rhodius, Medea invokes the Keres with songs and prayers, the Keres being chtonic daimones who are "devourers of the spirit, swift dogs of Hades which prowl through all the sky and are set upon mortal men".[8] With the aid of the Keres and the force of "her malevolent glances" she managed to kill the bronze man Talos. This implies that Medea had necromantic abilities and a personal power of her own – this matches with the concept of the Quimbanda Queen who reigns over spirits but is also powerful by herself.

> The strongest image of Medea in the ancient world was undoubtedly that of the witch, the sorceress using herbs, incantations and innate magical powers to achieve her aims. [...] the earliest sources, literary and artistic, show her as a dangerous magical figure. Her powers are not trivial – she can control natural forces, and even reverse the order of life and death by rejuvenating the old.[9]

The witch's cauldron was inherited by Quimbanda, of course. It is mentioned in several *pontos cantados*, the magical songs used to invoke the exus and the pombagiras:

---

8 Apollonius, and R. L. Hunter. *Argonautica*. Cambridge University Press, 2015.

9 Griffiths, Emma. *Medea*. Routledge, 2006.

| | |
|---|---|
| Ela é Maria, Ela é Maria, | She is Maria, She is Maria, She is |
| Ela é Maria, | Maria, |
| Ela é Maria | She is Maria |
| A chuva que cai do céu parece | The rain that falls from the sky |
| prata, | seems silver, |
| mulher que reina na terra é | woman who reigns on earth is you, |
| você, | There in the calunga she has |
| Lá na calunga ela tem poder, | power, |
| ela tem poder... | she has power ... |
| Mas ela faz caldeirão sem | But she makes the bottomless |
| fundo ferver! | cauldron boil! |

To help even more in the creation of our magical-mythical figure, Medea was also a queen. Different versions make her either a queen due to her marriage to Jason, or to the king of Athens, Aigeus, or by her own merit. Some variations have Medea marrying Achilles in the afterlife and living in the Elysium with him. *Post mortem* deification or daimonization for a few special souls was an important feature of ancient Greek beliefs, often tied to the hero cult – Achilles received hero cult and there are indications that Medea did also. The elevation of special souls after death survived the Christian revision of the afterlife to become a very important feature of Quimbanda, and here again Iberian witchcraft married harmoniously to the African traditions; invocations to Maria de Padilla in the Spanish spells came to Brazil via Portugal and refer to the concept that her soul was elevated and empowered by the Devil after she died. From the Bantu religion Quimbanda inherited the cult of the ancestors. With their family roots cut by the slave traffic, figures of a more mythical character were adopted in the Brazilian cults: old blacks, *caboclos*, *exus* and *pombagiras*. We will see that when we tell the story or the myth of the Queen of the Seven Crossroads.

# Hecate

Hecate appears in the variant genealogy of Medea which makes the sorceress the daughter of the goddess and sister (instead of niece) of Circe. As Medea is described as a priestess of Hecate, it is understandable that she shares in the iconographic associations of the goddess to the Moon, wild animals, and torches.

The genealogy of Hecate herself is clearly established in the *Theogony* of Hesiod, where she is the daughter of the Titans Perses and Asteria; later variations of the myth also made Hecate a deified mortal. In one version, the sacrificed Iphigenia is deified as Hecate by the goddess Artemis; in another, a nameless rude woman committed suicide after being transformed by Artemis into a dog and back. For Diodorus Siculus (first century BC), Hecate was a mortal queen who discovered the use of herbal drugs. In time, Hecate became a patroness of magic and sorcery; her rise to preeminence in these areas coincides with the appearance of the *goes* in Greece – the specialist in dealing with the souls of the dead. The goddess with these new attributions is very important for our understanding of the Queens of Quimbanda, as she encompasses the whole spectrum of ideas and powers later attributed to them.

[...] she is popularly described as a dread and mighty goddess ruling over the souls of the dead; she would instruct mortals in the art of magic, or send forth demons and spirits by night from the underworld, who dwelt in tombs or near the blood of murdered persons, or at the cross-roads (whence her name Trivia), and taught sorcery and witchcraft. When she appeared on earth she was accompanied by Stygian hounds, whose whining announced her approach; torches gleamed around her, and her hair was decorated with oaken boughs and serpents. In appearance she is described as either three-headed or three-bodied, being partly horse, partly dog, and partly lion or boar.[10]

Erotic magic from Greek-Roman culture was deeply connected to the souls of the dead; this is also an important feature of Quimbanda, where one of the most requested functions of the *pombagiras* is their help and advice on matters of sex and love. We have a very instructive example in the tale of Simaetha from Theocritus' second *Idyll*, where a woman tries to regain the affections of her former lover with a magical act performed at a three-way crossroads bordered by tombs. She addresses her prayer to the Triple Goddess of Crossroads:

So shine me fair, sweet Moon; for to thee, still Goddess, is my song, to thee and that Hecat infernal who makes e'en the whelps to shiver on her goings to and fro where these tombs be and the red blood lies. All hail to thee, dread and awful Hecat! I prithee so bear me company that this medicine of my making prove potent as any of Circe's or Medea's or Perimed's of the golden hair.[11]

Hecate in the *Theogony* is presented in such way that makes her concept comes close to the other crossroad deity also connected to the dead, Hermes. Hermes can travel to the three realms (Sky, Earth, and Hades), but Hecate has a share of power and honor over Sky, Sea, and Earth that later will extend also to Hades (her connection to the dead does not appear in the *Theogony*). Hesiod makes her "the crucial intermediary between

---

10 Ronan, Stephen. *The Goddess Hekate*. Chthonios, 1992.

11 Edmonds, J. M. (translator). *The Greek Bucolic Poets*, Heinemann, 1923.

gods and men"[12] and a deity that must be called "whenever anyone of men on earth offers rich sacrifices and prays for favor according to custom".[13]

Hesiod's catalogue of Hecate's powers, while not exhaustive, gives the impression of universality. But it is quite evident that these powers are not autonomous. Each area in which Hecate manifests her influence belongs either to a specific god (Poseidon, Hermes) or to a possible diversity of gods. Yet in each sphere her good will forms an essential ingredient of success – just as its absence seems to lead to failure.[14]

There is a lack of evidence that the Greeks, in their actual religious performances, did give Hecate the preeminence preached by Hesiod, but for us it is interesting that the Hesiodic Hecate comes very close to the African Eshu, the deity who is present everywhere, is favored by Olodumare (the higher deity) over the other orishas, must be propitiated first and whose favor is necessary for the success of any endeavor. Hecate in the *Theogony* was the one "whom Zeus the son of Cronos honored above all" and he made her the κουροτρόφος (a nurse of the young); "the goddess designated as *kourotrophos* was sometimes given the right of first sacrifice".[15]

Hecate and Eshu, of course, share their powers over the crossroads too.

---

12 Clay, Jenny Strauss, *The Hecate of the Theogony*, 1983.

13 Hesiod, and Hugh G. Evelyn-White. *Hesiod, the Homeric Hymns, and Homerica*. Heinemann, 1914.

14 Clay, Jenny Strauss, *The Hecate of the Theogony*, 1983.

15 Ibid.

# Intermezzo: One Example of the Amazing Power of Oral Traditions

The origins of Quimbanda are eminently oral, from both European and African roots. Although European culture was characterized by its high level of literacy, the transmission of its sorcerous and diabolical ideas which helped shape Quimbanda came to Brazil carried firstly by the illiterate witches exiled by the Portuguese Inquisition. As an impressive testimony to how ideas from the past could survive to blossom in the later Quimbanda, we have the following poetic sentence, to be found in many *pontos cantados* sung in the Quimbanda Terreiros in Brazil:

| | |
|---|---|
| De onde pombo gira vem | Where does pombo gira come from? |
| Aonde pombo gira mora | Where does pombo gira live |
| Ela mora na encruzilhada | She lives at the crossroads. |
| Onde o galo não canta | Where the cock does not sing |
| e criança não chora. | and child does not cry. |

I am making reference here to the verses "where the cock does not sing and child does not cry". David Jordan[16] attests that the same formula survives "today in traditional protective charms (*xorkia*) against the evil eye"[17] he found in Crete, Cephalonia and Athens, which he traced back first to "a sixteenth-century manuscript produced in southern Italy" and then to "a curious thin sheet of metal" found at Amorgos whose "orthography and vocabulary suggest the very early centuries of the Christian era":

The text is a prayer addressed to 'lady (kyria) Demeter, queen', written by or for a slave owner who begs her to

---

16 David Jordan is a member of the American School Of Classical Studies at Athens.

17 Jordan, David. "The Wretched Subject of Ancient Greek Magic." *Greek Magic: Ancient, Medieval And Modern*, June 2006.

curse someone who had induced the slaves to escape. The curse includes the words: 'May no child cry, no happy sacrifice be offered, no dog bark, no cock crow.'[18]

The formula survives to this day in Greece mixed with Christian prayers; in the aforementioned sixteenth-century manuscript it is the voice of Jesus Christ who threatens the demon of migraine: "[...] if you disobey me, there I shall destroy you in the burning mountain, where dog bays not and cock crows not". The poetic formula must have also survived in Spain and Portugal to be transmitted to Brazil, in an amazing instance of a magical verse crossing the centuries and countries. David Jordan's scholarly speculations indicate the possibilities of even further origins in time and space for it:

Here we see that the curse of 'dogs not barking, cocks not crowing' belongs to a tradition that spans two millennia. We can say a bit more. The goddess's title, 'lady (kyria)', is Eastern in origin, as students of Mediterranean religion have long recognized. Excavators on Delos, by unearthing another lead curse tablet, have provided a good illustration of this. Its text invokes (in Greek) the 'lady Dea Syria': she too is to punish a malefactor. The texts from Amorgos and Delos belong to a type of curse studied by the Dutch scholar H.S. Versnel, who characterizes them as 'prayers for justice'. The type is usually thought to have an Eastern background. Let me close with a speculation: could the motif of 'dogs not barking, cocks not crowing' belong to this Eastern background? Could it, in other words, be even older than its first recorded Greek instance, from Amorgos?

---

18 Jordan, David. "The Wretched Subject of Ancient Greek Magic." *Greek Magic: Ancient, Medieval And Modern*, June 2006.

# Aphrodite

Simaetha's magical operation also (very appropriately) mentions Aphrodite, goddess of love and sex. Aphrodite's connection to erotic magic (considered to be the province *par excellence* of the *pombagiras*) goes back to the *Iliad*, where she lends to the goddess Hera her κεστός ἱμάς (*kestos imas* = magical belt or girdle) "wherein are fashioned all manner of allurements; therein is love, therein desire, therein dalliance – beguilement that steals the wits even of the wise".[19] It is Aphrodite who in Pindar's *Fourth Pythian Ode* teaches Jason the use of the enchantment where a bird is bound to a rotating wheel, and instruct him "to be wise in prayers and charms" so he can set Medea's heart "afire with love."[20] The wheel is then used by Simaetha in her magical operation:

> As this puppet melts for me before Hecat, so melt with love, e'en so speedily, Delphis of Myndus. And as this wheel of brass turns by grace of Aphrodite, so turn he and turn again before my threshold.[21]

Although less prominent and well known, there is also a connection between Aphrodite and the crossroads:

> Each being is in itself a crossroads, where the various aspects of a person meet and fight each other. We know the triple aspects of Aphrodite: Uranian, Oceanian and

---

19 Homer, et al. *The Iliad*. Harvard University Press, 1924.

20 Pindar, and Ernest Myers. *The Extant Odes of Pindar. Translated into English with an Introd. and Short Notes by Ernest Myers*. Macmillan and Co., 1899.

21 Edmonds, J. M. (translator). *The Greek Bucolic Poets*. Heinemann, 1923.

Chthonian. She can be the modest goddess, the fecund goddess, the lecherous goddess. It is at the crossroads that She becomes the goddess of vulgar and impure love. Is it not curious to observe here that the Latin *trivium* means crossroads, and gave us the word *trivial*?

The goddess who lingers there, the Aphrodite of the crossroads, symbolizes the love of passage. She identifies with the goat she rides, in a sculpture of Skopas.[22]

Aphrodité Epitragia (Goat-Riding)
attributed to Skopas, Greek sculptor
from the 4th century BC

The vulgar side of Aphrodite's operations in the world understandably made her a patroness of prostitutes, and prostitutes

---

22 Chevalier, Jean, and Alain Gheerbrant. *Dictionnaire Des Symboles: Mythes, rêves, Coutumes, Gestes, Formes, Figures, Couleurs, Nombres.* R. Laffont, 1982.

in turn were considered to be magical practitioners or clients of magical practitioners. In a very agonistic society and trade, prostitutes resorted to magic to enhance their attractiveness and find good clients. This brings us again to the province of the *pombagiras*, whose myths and tales of origin frequently refer to years of prostitution before they died and their spirits were enlisted into the phalanx and legions of Quimbanda. In his monograph presented as a requirement to obtain a bachelor's degree in Social Sciences, Francisco Gleidson Vieira dos Santos interviewed practitioners of Umbanda and prostitutes, and from one *mãe-de-santo* he collected the following:

> For Dona Antônia Grande the Pombas-giras enter in any kind of magic, but they are more appropriate in the works of love. This characteristic is due to the fact that in life they were prostitutes, women much exploited by men and discriminated against by society. Possessing a very difficult life in this way, "then what they really want is to give love to people".[23]

The prostitutes interviewed explained their devotions and the magical exchange system they established with the *pombagiras*, with whom they had a very close, day-to-day interaction with the same aims and concerns of their predecessors in ancient Rome. In a kind of work where the client is desired and, at same time is feared, there is a great need for protection and assurance. In the poor prostitution zones of Brazil, Pombagira assumes the function held in Antiquity by other goddesses.

It is not the privilege of our culture to link a female deity to prostitution. Aphrodite, the Greek goddess of love,

---

23 A *Pomba-Gira no Imaginário das Prostitutas*, Francisco Gleidson Vieira dos Santos.

known and worshiped for her gifts of beauty, possessing more earthly references by the ancient Greeks, was known at Syracuse as Aphrodite of the Beautiful Buttocks, in Athens as Aphrodite the Courtesan, as well as at different times and places known like: Aphrodite of the hole or copulation, Aphrodite who rides Astride, which opens, the prostitute. Venus, the Roman version of the goddess of love and beauty, was considered the protector of prostitutes. In its conception as such was known as Venus Volgivava, and its festival was held annually on April 23, celebrated by prostitutes and male prostitutes.[24]

## Morgan le Fay

Coming closer to the genesis of Maria de Padilla as the Queen of Sorcery, we arrive at the elusive and dubious figure of Morgan le Fay. Morgan shares the duplicity of her antecessors, Circe and Medea, who were both friend and foe to the heroes. Circe had to be subjugated by Odysseus, with the help of Hermes, after trying to seduce and ensnare him as she did with his companions. Medea was the key to Jason's victory in the quest for the Golden Fleece, but later destroyed his life after his betrayal.

The first known version of Morgan is clearly of a mythological and benign character. In the *Vita Merlini* by Geoffrey of Monmouth she is the leader of a group of nine sisters who live and rule on the Island of Apples, "which men call The Fortunate Isle". She is a skilled healer and a shapeshifter who can transform herself into a bird. She receives the wounded king Arthur after his last battle, and promises to cure him if he can remain with her for enough time.

---

24 Gleidson Vieira dos Santos, Francisco. "A Pomba-Gira No Imaginário Das Prostitutas." Revista Homem, Tempo e Espaço, Sept. 2007.

*She was known to have studied magic while she was being brought up in the nunnery.*

Illustration of Morgan by William Henry Margetson,
for *Legends of King Arthur and His Knights* by Janet MacDonald
Clark, 1914.

She who is first of them is more skilled in the healing art, and excels her sisters in the beauty of her person. Morgen is her name, and she has learned what useful properties all the herbs contain, so that she can cure sick bodies. She also knows an art by which to change her shape, and to cleave the air on new wings like Daedalus; when she wishes she is at Brest, Chartres, or Pavia, and when she will she slips down from the air onto your shores. And men say that she has taught mathematics to her sisters, Moronoe, Mazoe, Gliten, Glitonea, Gliton, Tyronoe, Thitis; Thitis best known for her cither."[25]

The mythological resonances that can be discerned here are multiple, from Circe on her island, to the Muses, to the Hesperides, to the shapeshifting Great Queen of Irish mythology, the Phantom Queen or Queen of Phantoms, the Morrígan. Morrígan's relationship to the hero Cú Chulainn is also characterized by seduction, conflict, and danger. All of these feminine figures are, in fact, associated with danger to the hero, as even the gentle and innocent Hesperides have the help of a dragon to protect the Golden Apples. Seduction, conflict, and danger are also key elements in a relationship with the Queens of Quimbanda.

As the myth of Morgan developed through successive retellings, the dark side of the archetype began to manifest, as she "most often appears to take on an increasingly malevolent role in relation to Arthur", until she is turned into the "primary agent of mischief against him and his court".[26] But even when

---

25 Geoffrey, and John Jay. Parry. *The Vita Merlini*. University of Illinois, 1925.
26 Hebert, Jill M. *Morgan Le Fay, Shapeshifter*. Palgrave Macmillan, 2013.

QUEEN OF THE SEVEN CROSSROADS

cast in this final role, she is still the one who rescues Arthur in Avalon at the end of the story.

Brazilian culture, especially in the Northeast states, is deeply indebted to Chivalric romance. The Portuguese messianic myth called Sebastianism, for instance, is directly inspired by the idea that King Arthur did not die and will return to save the country. King Sebastian I of Portugal, who disappeared in 1578 in the battle of Alcácer Quibir, in the same fashion is believed to have survived to return in the future and save Portugal. He became an "encantado" in Brazil, an "enchanted being", a characteristic also given sometimes to the *pombagiras*. He is the spiritual protector of Lençóis Island in the state of Maranhão, where he manifests sometimes as a black bull with a star on his forehead. He keeps a large court ruling over other enchanted beings that manifest in trance rituals of healing, of which the most important are his "adopted daughters", three Turkish princesses who fled the war until they came to Brazil where they became enchanted spirits. In the "Encantaria do Tambor-de-Mina",[27] and in the Umbanda practiced in the states of the Amazon, they are known as the Three Sisters of the Sharp Tongue. Their names may vary according to place – Jarina, Rosalina and Mariana, or Jarina, Herondina and Mariana – and their functions overlap with the functions expected from *pombagiras*: Mariana executes works of prosperity and harmony, Jarina works of harmony and union of couples and families, and Herondina

---

27 Tambor de Mina is an Afro-Brazilian religious tradition, practiced mainly in the Brazilian states of Maranhão, Piauí, Pará and the Amazônia. *Tambor* means drum in Portuguese, and refers to the importance of the rhythmic element of worship. *Mina* derives from the name São Jorge da Mina, now also known as Elmina Castle, and refers to a designation given to African slaves, although the name did not necessarily refer to slaves who had passed through the fortress/port of São Jorge da Mina itself, but rather to "different ethnicities over time and place". (https://en.wikipedia.org/wiki/Tambor_de_Mina)

"is the only one who acts as an *exu* in the days of work of this line, guarding, protecting, opening the ways and executing the law, as well as all the good guardians, *exus* and *pombas-giras*".[28]

Their myths relate these enchanted kings and princess to the City of Aruanda, a spiritual paradise or refuge that echoes the legends of the Isle of Avalon.

## Iberian Sorceries

The following verses come from a process of the Spanish Inquisition from the first half of the 17ᵗʰ century. The professional sorcerer named as "Adriana" was acting on behalf of a client named Águeda de Herrera who wanted back the lover who had cheated on her, a man known as Blas Méndez.[29] Here we see the spirit of Maria de Padilla being invoked to help in the affairs of the heart in which she would excel four centuries later in the Quimbanda of Brazil.

28 "A Encantaria Amazônica Na Umbanda Parte II: As Três Irmãs Da Língua Ferina." Semeadura, https://www.semeadura.com/news/a-encantaria-amazonica-na-umbanda-parte-ii:-as-três-irmãs-da-lingua-ferina/.

29 Cañizares, Javier Fuentes. "En Torno a Un Antiguo Conjuro Mágico En Caló." *Revista De Folklore*, 2007, pp. 93–100.

| Así como esto yerbe, | As this boils, |
|---|---|
| Yerbe el corazón de Blas, | Boils the heart of Blas, |
| En el nombre de Satanás, | In the name of Satanás, |
| Y de Barrabás y del diablo | And from Barabbas and the devil |
| Cojuelo, | Cojuelo, |
| Y de su compañero | And from his partner |
| Y de la Jacarandina | And of the Jacarandina |
| Y de la Reina Sardina, | And from Queen Sardina, |
| Y de Doña María de Padilla | And from Doña María de Padilla |
| Y toda su cuadrilla, | And all her gang, |
| Y de Marta la que en los | And Martha the one who |
| infiernos está. | is in hell. |

The spirit of Maria de Padilla is not alone in the enterprise: besides her *cuadrilla*, she has with her two devils[30] (Satanás and the Cojuelo[31]); the soul of the Biblical Barabbas, the insurrectionist that the Jewish people chose to free instead of Jesus; and three other female spirits who greatly interest us here.

The *Jacarandina* makes reference to the *jácaras*, satirical songs from the Spanish Golden Age, a period of flourishing in arts and literature in Spain roughly inscribed between the end of the 15th century and the death of the writer Pedro Calderón de la Barca, in 1681. The *jácaras* dealt with popular characters called *jaques*, "malefactors, ruffians, bullies", and the women that

---

30 Perhaps three, depending on who is "his partner".

31 The Diablo Cojuelo (Lame Devil) is a legendary character from some parts of Spain. He is a devil who, far from being truly evil, is represented as the most mischievous spirit of hell, driving crazy his own demonic colleagues, who, to get rid of him, delivered him to an astrologer who had him locked in a glass vessel. It is also said that he is an inventor of dances, music and literature of picaresque and satirical character. Being one of the first angels to rise in heavenly rebellion, he was the first to fall to hell. The rest of his brothers landed on him, leaving him crippled and above all marked by the hand of God. That's where his nickname of Cojuelo comes from. (https://es.wikipedia.org/wiki/Diablo_Cojuelo)

cared for and supported them. The most popular *jácara* by the great writer Francisco de Quevedo was the *Jácara del Escarramán* (1612), a poem written as a letter from the *jaque* to his woman, "la Méndez":

> Of Escarramán we know that he is a hero of the *jacarandina* on which diverse *jácaras* were composed, sonnets, dances, etc.; de la Méndez, that she is the prostitute-lover-tributary-protégée of Escarramán, and we also know that Méndez is a surname that is associated burlesquely with a prostitute.[32]

So here we are again with the connection between erotic magic and prostitution, where the *Jacarandina* is most likely a pombagira type of spirit, a dead prostitute invoked in spells – maybe "la Méndez" herself. It is interesting also to note that in Quimbanda the *malandro*, similar to the Spanish *jaque*, is a type of spirit "invoked when his followers need help with domestic, business or financial matters and are reputed to be a worker of charity and the maker of good works".[33] They are often considered to be a kind of *exu*, the most famous being the spirit known as Zé Pelintra.

The *Reina Sardina* is most likely a corruption of *Regina Sardiniae*, the Queen of Sardinia. The Kingdom of Sardinia was initially comprised of the islands of Corsica and Sardinia, the *Regnum Sardiniae et Corsicae* that came under Spanish rule in 1297. Until the throne was passed to the Italian House of Savoy in the 18th century, the crown of the Kingdom of Sardinia passed through sixteen different heads. Fifteen of these monarchs

---

32 Osorio, Oscar. *"La Jácara del Escarramán de Quevedo"*. Letras Hispanas, Vol. 2, Issue 1, 2005.
33 "Zé Pelintra." Wikipedia, Wikimedia Foundation, Mar. 2020, pt.wikipedia.org/wiki/Zé_Pelintra.

were men, and at first glance any of them could have been the husband of the *Reina Sardina;* the list would be extensive as many of them had more than one wife. To be invoked in an erotic spell, however, the *Reina Sardina* should have been someone of note, as was Maria de Padilla – a popular figure somehow associated with sorcery or with the Devil. Luckily, one of the sixteen monarchs who received the crown as an inheritance and not by marriage *was* a woman, and what woman she was!

Joanna of Castile (1479 –1555), also known as *Juana la Loca* (Joanna the Mad), held the crown of the Kingdom of Sardinia from 1516 until her death. She was also officially the Queen of Castile, Aragon and Navarre, but spent most of her live secluded. Political uneasiness regarding Joanna started much earlier, as from the age of sixteen she showed signs of being skeptical regarding religious matters; when she was twenty-two (and already married and a mother of two) she resisted attending masses and confession. She was reputed to be very jealous of her husband, and after his premature death in 1506 her father and later, her son, had her imprisoned in the castle of Tordesillas until her death. Father and son took advantage of her history of jealousy and her excessive mourning to accuse her of madness.

The fact that Joanna was reputed as being "madly in love" with a husband who had not reciprocated her feelings and whom she believed was killed with poisons (the official record says he died of typhoid fever), was already enough to make her an apt candidate to be considered after her death a *pombagira* kind of spirit. But to that also must be added the necromantic undertones from her mourning behavior and a late attempt to exorcise her – which links her legendary life to the devil.

She wished to bury him in Grenada, in southern Spain, in order to establish him as the rightful king of the land that he never visited. She accompanied his body on the journey to make sure that it arrived safely since her father did not want Philip to have the recognition of being king in southern Spain. She would reportedly open his coffin and kiss his feet every day, though that is possibly a rumor. She did ensure that no other women were allowed in churches where she left his remains, leading many to speculate about her obsessive love. One of the chroniclers who followed her, Pietro Martire, wrote about "the same jealousy that tormented her during her husband's life." It seems that even in Philip's death his widow still loved her madly.[34]

The history of Joanna presents many of the ideas we see in the tales about the *pombagiras*, including persecution by a male figure: many stories about the *pombagiras* include a father or husband who mistreated them and forced them to live in the streets where they became prostitutes to survive. All of that would make the *Reina Sardina* a perfect candidate to be called upon in an erotic spell.

Then we have "Martha the one who is in hell". She is a popular figure in Spanish spells and one of the few that migrated to Brazilian witchcraft together with Maria de Padilla. She is often confused with Martha of Bethany, sister of Lazarus, who is venerated as a saint in the Roman Catholic Church. However, if we pay attention to what the spells really say, it is clear that originally there was a preoccupation to avoid the confusion:

---

34 Elkin, Bailey Grace (2017) *Madness in the Middle Ages: an Examination of the Treatment of the Mentally Ill in the Medieval Era Based on Order and Gender*. Undergraduate thesis, under the direction of Frances Kneupper from History, The University of Mississippi. 2017.

| Marta, Marta la diabla y | Martha, Martha the she-devil and |
|---|---|
| no la santa, y diablo cojuelo, | not the saint, and the lame devil, |
| traéme a fulano en el buelo y | bring me so-and-so in the bule and |
| diablo del horno traémelo en | devil of the oven bring him |
| torno.[35] | around. |

This Martha is not the saint, she is the "one who is in hell", the "she-devil and not the saint". But who really was she? The answer was in fact found by the folklorist Charles Godfrey Leland (the famous author of *Aradia, Gospel of the Witches*) in his research on the folklore of the Tuscany region of Italy, which he tied to ancient Etruscan and Roman pagan practices. In his work from 1892, *Etruscan Roman Remains in Popular Tradition*, he identified what he believed to be "by far the most prominent character in the popular mythology of Tuscany, or of that which is not Catholic", the spirit that "dwells in forests or fields" named "La Bella Marta" (The Beautiful Martha).

The Beautiful Martha received the epithet of *Madre del Giorno* (Mother of the Day) but was, according to Leland, paradoxically worshiped *by night*, which he attributed to "the fact that all spirits are connected with the old religion, now called witchcraft, and that its rites are conducted in secrecy and obscurity". One of the spells he recorded leaves no doubt that the "Martha who is in Hell" from the Spanish spells was adopted from the Italian folklore. There is nothing surprising about this interchange, as parts of southern Italy, together with Sicily and Corsica, were under the Crown of Aragon from the 15th to the 18th century.

---

35 Moliné-Bertrand, Annie. "Conjuros, oraciones y brujería en Castilla, siglos XVI y XVII", *Credencial Historia* No, 103.

## The Invocation of La Bella Marta by Night

*For this you should go into a wood or forest*
*at midnight and look at a star, and say*

Good evening, O Lady Martha;
I do not call thee Martha called of heaven,
I call upon the Martha named of hell.
Take these fine cloths
In the presence of ... (here the name is given).
Once he was so much my friend,
Now he is so much my foe:
May enemies and friends
All seem the same to him
Save me, his shining star.
I beat five fingers for him on the wall,
Five souls do I conjure,
Five priests, five friars,
Five damned souls,
Into the soul, into the life
Of . . .
May they pass into the life!
Bear this into his thoughts,
Drag him by beard and hair,
Drag him by remembrances of me!
If you will do this for me,
Three signs you will give me
A knocking at the door,
A dog barking,
A man whistling.
Should'st thou favorable be,
These three signs thou'lt grant to me !

Other Spanish conjures clearly mixed Saint Martha of Bethany with the "Beautiful Martha Named of Hell", as we can see in the following excerpt:

The spells belong to superstitious practices: they are made at night. In the process of Dona Maria de Vergara, the three women (herself, a niece of hers and a friend) would get up at eleven at night and stay awake until after one o'clock in the morning. A witness says that later "they closed in the room and lit all the lights". Doña María declares that they lit three yellow wax candles, saying that "the one was for the man she wanted to attract, another for the said Maria and the other for Sancta Marta, and she prayed for nine days to attract men to her will and said that there is nothing more valid than that prayer". It's about the spell of the star.[36]

The Spanish reference to the "spell of the star" also came from the Bella Marta tradition; the first spell we saw instructs the sorcerer to "go into a wood or forest at midnight and look at a star", and the next (also from Leland) identifies the Bella Marta with a star and also names her as a *queen*:

Beautiful Martha!
Beautiful Martha!
Beautiful Martha
Thou art beautiful as a star.
I come to behold you once more,
Once more to kneel before you,
That I may adore you better.
Midnight has struck,

---

36 Moliné-Bertrand, Annie. "Conjuros, oraciones y brujería en Castilla, siglos XVI y XVII", *Credencial Historia* No, 103.

I am kneeling before you;
Kneeling in a fair garden,
Where thou, beautiful Martha, art queen.

## From Spain to Brazil

Maria de Padilla and Martha from Hell (also named Martha the
Lost) were adopted by the Portuguese witches and figure in many
orisons and prayers. When the Portuguese Inquisition exiled
some of them to Brazil, the names of the spirits were carried with
them and soon started to appear in the records of the Inquisitorial
Visitations that happened between the last decades of the 16th to
the end of the 18th centuries.

That Maria de Padilla's image was already changing from
being merely one more spirit to be invoked in erotic spells to
an entity that received honors and with which some duty bonds
were established can be seen in an Inquisition process from 1673:

> She used to make a sign of Solomon, in which she the
> accused entered, and two chairs, by the side of the said
> sign of Solomon, and then she said certain words, and
> soon two shadows appeared, one of man and the other of
> woman, whom she said was Maria Padilha, with whom
> she spoke from the sign of Solomon, saying to her: Maria
> de Padilha, ask your lover Erasmo, by the torments he
> suffered for you, to do what I ask of you. And then she asked
> what she wanted. And soon the figure of Maria Padilha
> asked the other shadow which she said was Erasmo, to do
> what she asked. And the other shadow called, without
> being understandable, and soon an amount of pigs came,
> and between them a lame one, to whom the said shadow
> ordered what was asked to be done. And the accused kept

doing the practice to the said shadows during one hour, because if she did not do so they would beat her a lot.[37]

Maria de Padilla appears in this confession receiving honors (a chair to seat) and demanding a "practice" that should last at least one hour. The phalanx of spirits that attend the call of her "lover Erasmo" in the form of pigs reflect the passage in the Gospels where Jesus exorcised a legion of demons into pigs, but also reminds us of the men turned into pigs by Circe.

37 Meyer, Marlyse. *Maria Padilha e toda a sua quadrilha*. Livraria Duas Cidades. 1993.

‥◆‥

The name of Maria Padilha apparently was well established in the colony at least by the beginning of the 18th century, when it appears in the records of the Inquisition. That presence would be reinforced by the reception of the Portuguese *Book of Saint Cyprian* published in Lisbon by the Livraria Econômica at the end of the 19th century. This book has five spells where the name of Maria Padilha appears. The influence of the book in the milieu of the so called "low Spiritism" in Rio de Janeiro, where Quimbanda was being gestated, was very well attested by the Brazilian journalist João do Rio (1881-1921), who in 1904 conducted a series of interviews in the demimonde of Rio de Janeiro:

But what is ignored by the people who sustain the sorcerers, is that the base of their entire science is the *Book of Saint Cyprian*. The greatest alufas, the more complicated fathers-of-saint, have hidden between the stripes and the animals one less than fantastic edition of S. Cyprian. Whilst that crying creatures await for the bewitchings and the fatal mixtures the blacks spell the S. Cyprian, by the light of the lamps...[38]

The *Book of Saint Cyprian* also gave rise to another *pombagira* in Quimbanda, *Pombagira Bruxa de Évora*. Her statue depicts a crone riding a broom, with a simple red dress that half covers the left breast and leaves the other naked. A resumé of the general description given to her in *A Bruxa de Évora* by Farelli says:

---

38 Rio, João do. "As Religiões no Rio". Coleção Biblioteca Manancial n.º 47. Rio de Janeiro, Editora Nova Aguilar. 1976.

The Witch of Évora was Moorish, raised in Iberia, spoke Latin, Arabic, and Portuguese well; was created by an old aunt who had taught her the art of spells, giving her as talisman seven gold coins of the caliph Omir, an Agatha Stone with inscriptions in Arabic and a silver plate bearing the name of the prophet. The Arabian Witch was called Crooked Moorish, wore rags, but on her breast shone an Amber amulet. She read the Qur'an and wrote, knew Mathematics and looking at the stars knew how to recognize them, did spells and cures. She knew the magic of her Muslim ancestors, but living in the thirteenth century also presented knowledge of Celtic culture. She was always visited by a black goat.

The curious thing is that, as the eminent Portuguese Cyprianist José Leitão clarified for me, the editors of the *Book of Saint Cyprian* borrowed the tale of the Witch of Evora from a work published in 1739 entitled *História das Antiguidades de Évora*, written by the Portuguese scholar Amador Patrício. The Witch of Evora is representative of another literary trend, Roman instead of Greek, which portrayed the witch not as a beauty of ambivalent character but as a hag prone to satisfying her horrible lusts. The Roman witches described by authors like Horace (Canidia and Sagana), Petronius (Oenothea), Lucan (Erictho), and Apuleius (Meroe, Pamphile, and Photis) all follow this stereotype and helped to create the image of the witch that would develop with the Inquisition.

Évora was one of the six seats of the Inquisition in Portugal, together with Lisbon, Coimbra, Tomar, Porto, and Lamego. There was also a Tribunal established at Goa (India), but the visitations of the Inquisition in Brazil were under the auspices of the Lisbon tribunal. The Portuguese Inquisition was much more concerned in finding crypto-Jews and was very lenient toward other accusations. There were few executions of witches and often they were exiled to the colonies, such as Brazil. If we go through the records of the Portuguese Inquisition, we can produce a portrait of the kind of activities these witches carried to Brazil which helped to create Quimbanda. The following list was first published in my study "The Gnosis of the Devil", found in *NOXAZ: Primal Current* (The Black Serpent Series Book 1).

**Place:** The invocations were usually done in the fields or bushes, sometimes in the backyard of the house. The domestic space could be dangerous to other people (as the demons could attack them) and to the witch herself (who could be spied upon and denounced), but some witches believed the spirits could manifest better in the isolated places.[39]

*"Margarida Pimenta, concretely, said to a client that she could not do anything at the house of her sister named Calista because there was a boy there [...] son of the said Calista and she was afraid that the demons could do him some harm and she would instead do it in the fields because there the demons came to her better."*[40]

**Time:** The chosen days were the Fridays, the Wednesdays and the Mondays, usually between the twenty and two and midnight hours.[41]

---

39 Bethencourt, Francisco. O imaginário Da Magia: Feiticeiras, Adivinhos e Curandeiros Em Portugal. No século XVI. Companhia Das Letras, 2004. *Inferno Atlântico - Demonologia e Colonização nos Séculos XVI-XVIII*, Laura de Mello e Souza.

40 Inquisition of Evora, process 6492, Page 18r-v. Quoted by Francisco Bethencourt.

41 Bethencourt, Francisco. O *imaginário Da Magia: Feiticeiras, Adivinhos*

**Protection:** Some witches used simple variations of the magical circles we know from the grimoires, usually drawing a simple circle, a sign of Solomon or a cross in which they went inside.

*Isabel Lopes, for example, used to say that she would make in the house a wheel and would go into it and from inside it she would call the devils, who if they found her out of that wheel and the sign of Solomon would make her in pieces. In a confession of Iria Jorge, she said that the devil always challenged her to leave the circle she had drawn on the floor, because that way she would be under his power.*[42]

**Nudity:** Partial nudity and loose or disheveled hair is frequently mentioned, and was even considered by some to be a very necessary condition (see below the justification of the witch Margarida Pimenta).

*"To walk naked and with the hair [loose or disheveled] certainly identified, in the popular imagination, the protagonist of this act with the witch. In the XVI century, in Evora, it is known that the person interested in the conjuration of the stones should do it 'with [loose] hair and in shirt, gazing at a star and holding in the hand nine stones taken from crossroads'. In the XVII century, such gestures persisted: in 1637, Maria Ortega conjured the spirits disheveled and naked from the waist up, and in 1664 it was in an identical form that Maria da Silva invoked demons or uttered a beautiful orison of Saint Erasmus, using also one bowl and green candles."*[43]

---

*e Curandeiros Em Portugal.* No século XVI. Companhia Das Letras, 2004.

42 Ibid.

43 Mello e Souza, Laura. *Inferno atlântico: Demonologia e colonização,*

**Offerings:** There is frequent mention of simple offerings, generally of food, made to the spirits.

*Margarida Pimenta, who put outside the circle three small portions of barley for when the demons under the figure of piglets came, justified the failure of her conjuration saying that she was not naked and lacked the entrails of a goat to feed them. Brites de Figueiredo, for her part, was famous for giving bread, meat and fish to a little devil named Martinho; [the devil's preferred] according to Simão Pinto "black bread and fish cooked with mud"; Brites Dias gave them garlic and onions to eat."* [44]

**Conjure:** The conjuration is made with simple verses, easily remembered and repeated.

**Aims:** The invocations of demons are usually made to solve quotidian problems and often on behalf of clients.

**Relationship:** The relationship with the devils may vary; some witches brag about their power over the spirits, others confess their submission and fear and often the dangers of the activity are also mentioned.

*"Now the [witch known as] Arde-lhe-o-rabo[45] used to affirm to wander disheveled and naked in the churchyards and bushes, in search of sorceries: "because I go at midnight to my*

---

*séculos XVI-XVIII.* Companhia das Letras. 1993.

44 Bethencourt, Francisco. *O imaginário Da Magia: Feiticeiras, Adivinhos e Curandeiros Em Portugal.* No século XVI. Companhia Das Letras, 2004.

45 *Arde-lhe-o-rabo* is a vulgar expression which translates roughly to "Her-ass-burn".

*backyard with the head in the air and the door opened toward*
*the sea and I bury and unbury some jars and I am naked from*
*the waist up and with the hair* [disheveled] *and I speak with*
*the devils and call them and I am with them in great danger."*
*When she returned from these walks, she came "beaten" by*
*the devils and the works she had.*[46]

We should pay special attention to the way these witches
confessed to practice their crafts: naked from the waist up and
with loose hair. We find this also in their Spanish counterparts.
This is how the great majority of the images of *pombagiras* sold in
Brazil represent these entities.

All that we've seen so far shows the ever-flowing concepts
that go from *magic to myth*, and then again from *myth to magic*.
Behind the Circes and Medeas and the ugly Roman hags hide
real people, real witches whom the poets adapted in different
ways to their literary efforts. Doing this, they altered the reality
of the practices and the image of the practitioners. In a second
moment, however, the poems, epics and novels influenced the
imagination of later practitioners. This is how Maria de Padilha
was associated with sorcery in the *Romanceros*, but afterward
entered into the spells of real witches. The Witch of Évora began
her career as a literary creation but ended as a *pombagira* called to
work in very real rituals of magic.

## Biblical Characters

Several characters from Jewish-Christian mythology helped
create the figure of the Witch in the West, and by extension

---

46 Mello e Souza, Laura. *Inferno atlântico: Demonologia e colonização,
séculos XVI-XVIII.* Companhia das Letras. 1993.

had some direct or indirect impact on the development of the *pombagiras*.

To begin, we have the first woman herself, Eve. Her interaction with the Serpent caused her to be considered, in fact, as the first witch. The Kabbalah of the Zohar in the 13th century was not shy in blaming her for the sexual nature of their interaction, and assumed that the "venon" of the Serpent spoiled Eve and was transmitted to all subsequent generations, this "venon" being the source of women's powers of witchcraft. The nature of Eve, and of women in general, was then forever associated with sin, the demonic, disobedience and a rupture with the divine.[47]

As if Eve wasn't already evil enough, Jewish legends during the Middle Ages elaborated upon an insignificant mention in the Book of Isaiah (34:14) to create the figure of the rebellious first wife of Adam, Lilith. Lilith had an extraordinary career, being raised in the Kabbalah to the level of a Queen of Hell and consort of the Devil. As the Kabbalah gained momentum in Spain up to the Expulsion of the Jews in 1492, the idea of Lilith as wife to Samael may have had some impact on the Iberian spells where the main devils are mentioned with their "wives". Nowadays, there are Quimbandeiros who identify the Pombagira Queen of Hell with Lilith.

Other Biblical characters later associated with witchcraft and/or undesirable female behavior (two things often conflated, and that represent fundamental aspects of the *pombagira*'s concept) were the Queen of Sheba, Jezebel, Herodias (mother of Salome), and (obviously) the Witch of Endor. As we will see, the Queen of Sheba is considered to be, in some of Quimbanda's myths, one of the incarnations of the Queen of the Seven Crossroads.

---

47 Ribeiro, Silvana Mota. "Ser Eva e dever ser Maria : paradigmas do feminino no cristianismo." RepositóriUM, Celta, 1 Jan. 1970, hdl. handle.net/1822/5357.

From the New Testament we have the figure of Mary Magdalene, who also influenced greatly the conception of the *pombagira*. As she was later (erroneously) considered to be a penitent ex-prostitute, she became the perfect example of the *pombagiras* who abandon the darkness and become "baptized" exus working for the Umbanda. A mention in Luke 8:2 connected Mary Magdalene with the devil and is often associated with the epithet given to the *pombagira* as "the wife of seven husbands":

> And certain women, which had been healed of evil spirits and infirmities, Mary called Magdalene, out of whom went seven devils.[48]

'Mary Magdalene',
Andrea Solario and Bernardino Luini (ca. 1524 AD)

---

48 The Bible. Authorized King James Version. Luke 8:2.

———— •◆• ————

The African slave trade to Brazil operated from 1514 to 1850, when the last ship *Duas Clementinas* landed the 444 survivors from the original 490 shipped at the port of Benguela.[49] Three main African areas provided slaves for three distinctive regions in Brazil: the Amazonian captaincies received most slaves from the Upper Guinea; Rio de Janeiro and the southern areas from Angola; and Bahia and Pernambuco drew slaves mostly from the Bight of Benin.[50]

The most numerous and culturally significant groups were the West African Yoruba taken to Bahia and the Bantu people mostly distributed in Rio de Janeiro. Rio de Janeiro was the final destination of the ship *Duas Clementinas*. Both cultures helped shape Quimbanda, and it is important to know some essential facts about their religious beliefs and practices.

## Yoruba Religion

Both cultures contributed to the genesis of Quimbanda. The Yorubas[51] believe in a supreme deity, called Olorum or Olodumare, who created the world but remains inaccessible and

49 http://www.slavevoyages.org/voyage/900234/variables
50 *From Africa to Brazil: Culture, Identity, and an Atlantic Slave Trade, 1600–1830,* Walter Hawthorne.
51 We should note that "Yoruba" is an overall identity imposed from the outside and never fully accepted by the peoples it indicates. The Haussa neighbors gave the name to the inhabitants of the city of Oyó and the missionaries used it to facilitate their linguistic efforts.

does not receive cult. Between humans and this more exalted and unachievable deity we find the Orishas, which represent the practical aspect of the religion. The Orishas preside over different aspects of the world and over different offices. They also have a special relationship with the individual, who is considered to be the "daughter" or the "son" of one Orisha who "rules over the head" of the person. An individual pre-ordained destiny is ascribed to each one before birth, and its fulfillment is the main reason to live. They believe in reincarnation as a positive thing, though bad people and suicides may be barred from reincarnation and suffer in a separate place called the Orun-Apade (Place of Potsherds).

To navigate through life and fulfill destiny the Yoruba religion establishes contact and guidance with the Orishas by means of a complex and very rich system of divination, the Ifá, and by spiritual possession during religious ceremonies. It is a very practical religion, focused on ethical behavior and on a system of offerings and sacrifices that aim to correct the path of the devotee. This is worked through manipulations in the web of the energy that permeates everything, the *ashé*, the sacred life force not just possessed by both gods and men, but present everywhere. The quality and the strength of the *ashé* varies according to the time, the space and whatever possesses it.

There are two main kinds of Orishas: *primordial divinities*, which existed before men and even before the creation of the natural world, and *deified ancestors*, important and singular people from the beginnings of human history who achieved the status of Orisha after their deeds and way of death – like the great king *Sango* who hung himself. It is important for us to know that these deified ancestors *have tales about them* – just like the *exus* and *pombagiras* of Quimbanda. It is also of note that for many, Maria Padilha is being elevated to the rank of Orisha.

Below the deified Orishas we have the ancestors venerated by their families, or in a more general and public way in a cult that address them in a collective form – like in the cult of the *Egumgum*. Not all the dead, however, achieve the state of postmortem veneration. They are elected by Olodumare when they have fulfilled three essential conditions: lived a good life, attained old age, and left descendants. The main thing about the ancestors is that they are *sources of power to the living*: they care for and protect their families and mediate between them and the Orishas. However, if angered, they can be a source of misfortune.

It is a common practice among Quimbandeiros to say that "the ones who protect me do not sleep". This is related to the Yoruba belief that "witches and sorcerers cannot harm a man and bad medicine cannot have effect on him if his ancestors are not asleep";[52] that is why the Yorubas say to their ancestors "Baba mi ma sun lorun" – "my father, do not sleep in heaven".[53]

## Bantu Beliefs

The word "bantu" is an artificial creation which comes from the German linguist Wilhelm Bleek, made popular after the publication of his 1862 book *A Comparative Grammar of South African Languages*. Proposing the existence of a Proto-Bantu language that diversified over time into more than 2000 different dialects, Bleek used the prefix *ba ("people") and the root *ntu ("some, any") to create a neologism meaning "the people".

Subjacent to the common etymological field we find a bedrock of religious concepts also shared by this large group, of which the two main elements are the Supreme Being, the source of life and

52 Ige, Abiodun. (2006). "The Cult Of Ancestors In African Traditional Religion." An Encyclopaedia of The Arts. 10. 26.
53 Ibid.

order (Nzambi, Kalunga, Zambi, Lessa, Mvidie, Mulungu) and the ancestors and antecedents.[54] The ancestors are the ancient founders, whose memories lost their particularities, whilst the antecedents are family members deceased, usually counting to three or four generations past.

Not as important as the dead, there were also tutelary spirits of nature who inhabited lakes, rivers, rocks, winds, forests or material objects. The ancestors, the "great dead", were considered founders of communities by having signed the first alliances with these spirits of nature, but sometimes these nature spirits were confused with the ancestors themselves.[55]

The Bantu shared many similarities with the Yoruba, including the conception of life as *force*; everything is understood as being the result of interactions of the different forces that all came from the Supreme Being. As the Supreme Being remains aloof, the intermediation and intercessions are left to the ancestors and the antecedents. Here is where Bantu and Yoruba had their main differences, and the lack of a divine intermediary hierarchy and the focus on the practices related to the dead led to a depreciation of the Bantu culture in comparison to the Yoruba, perpetrated by both Catholic religious and academic researchers.

When the Portuguese came to Western Africa, both the Yoruba and the Bantu had already organized several royal states, such as the Kingdom of Kongo, the Lunda Empire, and the Luba Empire of Angola. As we are going to see, Quimbanda is considered to be mostly derived from the Bantu cults of ancestors, in which dead Kings and Queens had great importance:

> Just as first settlers continued to watch over their communities, so dead kings and queens continued to

---

54 In Portuguese we say "ancestrais" e "antepassados", respectively.

55 *A religião dos bantos: novas leituras sobre o calundu no Brasil colonial*, Robert Daibert.

oversee their realms. These royal spirits were often associated with regional shrines. While Bemba kings were buried in one royal cemetery, rulers elsewhere were buried at their capitals. Since each ruler built a new capital, royal shrines were widely scattered. Initially the royal shrine was cared for by retired officers of the dead king and by royal widows; the office then became hereditary to their descent lines. The dead ruler might also speak through a medium attached to the shrine, a medium whose post was not usually hereditary. Periodically the living king or queen sent offerings to all the royal shrines throughout the kingdom to invoke the protection of the new ruler. Their anger at his bodily failure or neglect could bring disaster upon the realm.[56]

Contact with the spirits was intermediated by the *mediums*; although some aspects of their religious practices were performed by priests and priestesses, the "spirit-through-medium" ordinances topped them: the spirits "gave demands and warnings, chided earth priests and priestesses for ritual neglect or abandonment of ancestral ways, called for new shrines to be built, instigated changes in routines, and demanded offerings for themselves and their medium".[57]

Another interesting feature we see replicated in Brazilian Quimbanda is the popularity given to certain spirits:

Some territorial shrines served only a neighborhood, while others served a large region as places of last appeal.

---

56 Thomson, Gale. "Central Bantu Religions." Encyclopedia of Religion, Encyclopedia.com, 26 Dec. 2019, https://www.encyclopedia.com/environment/encyclopedias-almanacs-transcripts-and-maps/central-bantu-religions.

57 Ibid.

Shrines might be interlinked because they were associated with the same spirit, or because mediums in many places claimed possession by the same spirit. The most famous spirits had many mediums. When nearby shrines and mediums failed to give satisfaction, communities sent delegations to distant shrines and mediums, crossing linguistic and political boundaries. This gave witness that in the last analysis all shared the same human interests. Homogenization of belief and rituals was inevitable.[58]

## Drums of Affliction

The mediumistic practice of the African Bantus was open to innovations; the spirits working with the medium could "sometimes announce the arrival of previously unknown spirits".[59] Not always, however, did the coming of a new spirit happen through the established practice of the medium; spirits known as *mahamba* or *masabe* could afflict normal people with illnesses by seizing upon or entering their victims. The afflicted person is then forced to look for a *masabe* cult where the spirit is identified according to specific songs played on the drums. The victim will feel compelled to dance to the correct song and afterwards start to learn how to interact with the spirit that becomes her protector.

Cults of suffering, or of affliction as Victor Turner called them, may have been of minor importance prior to the

---

58 Thomson, Gale. "Central Bantu Religions." Encyclopedia of Religion, Encyclopedia.com, 26 Dec. 2019, https://www.encyclopedia.com/environment/encyclopedias-almanacs-transcripts-and-maps/central-bantu-religions.

59 Ibid.

QUEEN OF THE SEVEN CROSSROADS

twentieth century. During that century, however, these cults proliferated. They are based on the belief that various kinds of spirits seize upon or enter human victims, who then must come to terms with them. Treatment requires identification of the spirit and instruction in how to meet its demands. Thereafter the sufferer becomes an adept able to treat new victims. All adepts in the locality are expected to help their fellow sufferers, and this joins them in a ritual community. As the people of surrounding areas become suspicious that the new spirit has begun work in their community, adepts are summoned to diagnose and treat, and so the cults spread rapidly.[60]

I want to mention a case reported by the German anthropologist Thomas G. Kirsch in his book *Spirits and Letters: Reading, Writing and Charisma in African Christianity*; it is the case of Christian woman from Zambia who "suffered from a severe illness until she started to attend a *masabe* cult". The cult leader performed a divination using verses from the Bible to identify the spirit and its song. When the song was performed by the drummers she felt compelled to dance. She became healthy and sane as she joined the cult and started to receive more spirits. The spirits identify not only with a specific song or rhythm, they also ask for specific dressing. Her first spirit required she use white and red cloths with white, black and red beads.[61]

---

60 Thomson, Gale. "Central Bantu Religions." Encyclopedia of Religion, Encyclopedia.com, 26 Dec. 2019, https://www.encyclopedia.com/environment/encyclopedias-almanacs-transcripts-and-maps/central-bantu-religions.

61 *A Study of Religious Processes among the Ndembu of Zambia*, V.W. Turner.

People acquainted with the rituals of Quimbanda will immediately identify several common features here: many mediums are forced by spirit-illnesses and other problems to join the Umbanda or the Quimbanda, such as the Zambian woman; the *exu* or the *pombagira* that possesses the medium has to be identified; after the identification, the medium starts to use a cloth appropriate to the spirit and the spirit is served with its proper drinks and foods; each spirit attends and is called to the ceremony by a specific *ponto cantado* (song); often it is the reaction of the medium to the *ponto cantado* that helps identify the spirit.

Let's keep all this in mind when we see the myth of Zelio de Moraes and the foundation of Umbanda in the next chapter.

—————— •◆• ——————

We are going to start our pursuit of a better understanding of the origins and features of Quimbanda by looking at some etymological clues.

Of great importance to us is the work published in 1894 by the Swiss linguist, Protestant missionary, and anti-slavery activist Héli Chatelain (1859-1908). During his stay in Angola he learned the *Kimbundu* language well enough to produce a *Kimbundu Grammar* published in 1888. The book we are making reference to here is his *Folk-Tales of Angola*, a work remarkable because it was published in a bilingual format, with the original words he wrote down from his informants. From these tales we can glimpse who the original *kimbandas* were and what they did according to the folk traditions that survived into the 19th century.

The first tale where a *kimbanda* appears is the one the entitled *Nianga dia Ngenda and his dogs*. Nianga dia Ngenda is a hunter who suddenly became unsuccessful in his hunting, and looked for a *kimbanda* for help. Chatelain here translates *kimbanda* as "medicine-man"; in his previous *Grammar* he indicates its meanings as "*curandeiro*, native doctor". The medicine-man "prepared a medicine": Chatelain translated the word "*umbanda*" as "medicine". To work well, the *umbanda* has a *ijila*, a prescription to be observed.

A *kimbanda* appears again in the tale *King Kitamba kia Xiba*. King Kitamba loses his head-wife Queen Muhongo, and imposes on his village a dire and untraditional mourning that will last unless the dead queen is brought back. Powerless to sort out the situation, the elders seek the help of the *kimbanda* (here translated as "medicine-man" and "doctor"); they ask the *kimbanda* to go to the *ku'Alunga* to fetch the dead queen.

Chatelain transliterated *ku'Alunga* as *Kalunga* in the English version of the tale. In his *Grammar* he translated *Kalunga* as "*mar, sea*"; in the *Folk-Tales* he expands the meanings to: "(1) death; (2) the personification of death in the shape of the king of the nether world, called Kalunga-ngombe, and the world of shades itself; (3) the ocean; (4) an interjection of wonder; (5) a title of respect, given to a chief, and, among the Imbangala, to every freeman of some importance".

The *Kalunga* in the tales is the underground realm of the dead *accessible through the graves*. The *kimbanda* in the tale of King Kitamba asked to be buried alive so he could enter the *Kalunga*; he succeed in finding the dead queen, but she explained to him that in the *Kalunga* "never comes one here to return again". She pointed to a seated figure and said: "He is Lord Kalunga-ngombe; he is always consuming us, us all". Then she instructed the *kimbanda* that he could not eat there if he wished to return to the world of the living.

In this tale a road appeared to the *kimbanda* when he was buried alive; in the tale *Sudika-Mbandi*, the semi-divine hero child who gives his name to the story, is betrayed and is also buried alive; like the *kimbanda* when inside the grave "there he found a road" which took him to the kingdom of *Kalunga-ngombe*, o Rei da Kalunga. He asked to marry the daughter of *Kalunga-ngombe*, but failed in one of the tests and was swallowed by a crocodile. His younger brother went after him, accused his killers and demanded that they uncover the grave. He entered the grave, found the road and succeeded in retrieving the bones of his elder brother from the belly of the crocodile and resurrected him.

How could someone become a *kimbanda*? In the tale *The Young Man and The River*, a "young man [who] was given as a pledge by his uncle" became a permanent slave after his uncle and the rest of the family died. He was beaten, dressed in rags and received the usual mistreatment reserved for slaves in African societies. He was helped by the spirit of the River, who came to him in dreams and instructed him to retrieve a *ngonga-basket* from the river in the morning. The basket had "medicine-things [umbanda] all complete in it".

He dreams (that) they are showing him the plants of medicine, saying, "When thou goest to cure such diseases, the plants are such. Whoever has sores, his plant is such a one. The medicine of chiefs, thou shalt make it this way and this way." They are silent; he wakes up: a dream.

The slave became a *kimbanda* with the help of spirits that communicated with him through dreams. As a very successful *kimbanda*, he was able to buy his freedom and become rich.

What can we infer from these tales, as we again try to follow the path that goes from magic to myth, and from myth to magic? A few things:

1. The *kimbanda* could provide magical solutions for daily problems by preparing *umbandas*.
2. The *kimbanda* could access the dead or the realm of the dead, maybe through a practice of incubation where he enacted a self-burial, or slept over a grave.
3. The *kimbanda* acted as a healer.
4. One of the ways the *kimbanda* could receive instructions from the spirits was through dreams.
5. The *kimbanda* was seen in a very positive light.
6. The *kimbanda* was an office that could be very lucrative.

What we do not see in these tales is the *kimbanda* being possessed by spirits in his craft. In a note, however, Chatelain implies that there are two different kinds of *kimbanda*; it is not clear if only the first kind (*kimbanda kia dihamba*) is possessed, while the second (*kimbanda kia kusaka*) is merely a doctor. The story *The Young Man and The River* indicates that both had spirit help.

When an Angolan has suffered wrong, he goes and lodges a complaint before a judge of his choice, or before the chief of the tribe (as repeatedly described in these stories), or he resorts to the spirits, and calls on them for redress, often also for the punishment of the culprit. For this purpose, he goes to some one who is known as being possessed of this or that spirit, and lays the case before him, or rather, through him before the spirit he represents. Then the spirit is asked to either restore the stolen object, or force the debtor to pay, or to visit the murderer or ill-treater with death or sickness, and so forth. The spirit's medium listens gravely to the adjuration, but says nothing in reply. Sometimes the adjuration is, as in the present case, simply a kind of affidavit, either to prove one's innocence, when accused, or to prove one's right to complain. The medium receives a reward only in case the object in view is attained. Such a medium is *kimbanda kia dihamba*, as distinguished from the *kimbanda kia kusaka*, or physician who cures diseases. The act of bringing some evil on a real or imaginary offender through the medium of a spirit is called *ku-loua*. This *ku-loua* in self-defence is lawful, but the secret use of spirits for killing or hurting others, which is called *ku-loua pulu* (bewitching), constitutes the greatest crime a man can be guilty of, and is invariably punished with death. The witch or wizard is called *muloji*.

# Winds of the Dead

As a good example of the interplay between magic and myth, we have the story of Luzia Pinta, native of Angola, taken as a slave to Brazil in the beginning of the 18th century. Just as with the young man of the folktale who was helped by the spirit of the River, Luzia Pinta was taken by the spirits that previously belonged to her aunt. The spirits of the dead brought to her "winds of divination". She engaged in the practice known in colonial Brazil as *calundu*, rituals of dance and spiritual possession where the spirits prescribe medicines and spells to help the afflicted; she also became rich enough to buy her freedom and to own slaves herself.

The origin of the term *calundu* is considered to be the word *kilundu*, which in Angola meant a spirit or inhabitant of the invisible world.[62] Like the young man from the tale she was chosen by the spirits, but like the Zambian woman with the *mahamba* she was forced by them into the craft. Part of her office was to help release other people affected by bad spirits, but works for love and fortune or to separate or bring together people were also part of the rituals of the *calundus*. She was not alone in this fate: there is enough information for us to know that the *calundus* were widespread and were frequented by people of both African and European origins, slaves and free. The description of another practitioner, a slave named Branca, also from the beginning of the 18th century, gives us a clear idea about the ceremonies of the *calundus*:

The presence of the offering and the sacrifice can best be observed in the calundu of the slave Branca, in Bahia, who at the beginning of the eighteenth century entered

---

62 Kilundu, sub. – Espírito; Ser do mundo invisível. In *Dicionário kimbundu-português, linguístico, botânico, histórico e corográfico. Seguido de um índice alfabético dos nomes próprios*, Assis Junior (1887- 1961).

into trance and offered healing to those who attended her rituals. Under the touch of musical instruments, such as canzás and tabaques, she often danced and sang in the "language of Angola" invoking her dead relatives. [...] Branca's calundu was guided by the same basic principles of the Central African rituals bantos. She used marks made with a white clay called mpemba on her body or face to facilitate her access to the world of the dead, where the ancestors who were supposed to possess her lived. It was believed that the dead left their bodies and migrated to the mpemba, underground world of white clay. Thus, this substance came to be considered the symbol of the benevolent dead, and was therefore widely used as an element of protection among the Central Africans.[63]

The "white clay called mpemba" evolved into the special piece of chalk known today as "pemba", used to mark (usually on the floor) the magical signs called "pontos riscados" that identify, invoke and help to manifest the spirits of Quimbanda. We see that on the *calundus* the marks were made not on the floor, on the walls or over objects, but on the skin of the medium, helping through sympathetic action the contact with the dead.

## The Macumba of Juca Rosa

The real story of Luzia Pinta did not have a happy ending like the previous folktale we saw. Her success was the cause of her downfall as she caught the attention of the Inquisition, was arrested, sent to Lisbon, tortured and then exiled to the Algarves,

---

63 A *religião dos bantos: novas leituras sobre o calundu no Brasil colonial*, Robert Daibert.

the southernmost region of Portugal. Almost two centuries later, in the last decades of the 19<sup>th</sup> century, a religious leader with a set of very similar practices fell, not to the Church, but to the State: his name was José Sebastião da Rosa, popularly known as Juca Rosa. Juca Rosa's great success caught the attention of the police and he was arrested, prosecuted and sentenced to six years in jail.

The story of Juca Rosa is of great importance because it provides key information about the practices of the Macumba of Rio de Janeiro, the Macumba being the main source of both the Umbanda and the Quimbanda of the 20<sup>th</sup> century. Juca's ritual was clearly of Bantu structure, although it adopted many elements from the Christian Catholic religion. He was a Brazilian free man born to an Angolan slave mother, the mother most likely being the source of his religious performance. In the ceremonies he was possessed to the sound of the *macumbas*, the percussion instruments that inspired the name of the many similar practices that existed then in Rio de Janeiro. The main spirit to possess him was called Pai Quimbombo (Father Quimbombo), a spirit of which it was said that he could do "both good and evil". As we saw, the original Bantu concept of an ancestor bringing good or bad fortune was related to the conduct of the living members of the family; with Juca Rosa, however, we see that the expression "both good and evil" indicates the predisposition of the spirit to attend good and bad requisitions from the clients of the medium. The expression would become one of the key indicators of the *exus* and *pombagiras* in opposition to the other categories of spirits that only do good works.

Words known to be used for the religious leader of the *macumbas*, like *mbanda*, *umbanda* and *quimbanda* are all indicative of the Bantu origin of the practice.[64] The *Dicionário*

---

64 *Religiões Negras No Brasil: Da escravidão à pós-emancipação*, edited by Valéria Gomes Costa, Flávio Gomes.

*Kimbundu-Português*[65] has *kimbanda* as "person who treats the sick; magician; exorcist; necromancer; witch";[66] and *umbanda* as "witchery; magic; art or way to enchant, to heal".[67] The name "macumba" apparently was initially given by outsiders to the cults after the use of the musical instruments with that name, but it was adopted at some stage by the practitioners themselves; Juca Rosa, for instance, was known as the King of the Macumbas. Chatelain in one of his notes gave a more detailed description of the original Bantu meaning of these terms:

*U-mbanda* is derived from *ki-mbanda*, by prefix u-, as u-ngana is from ngana. Umbanda is: (i) The faculty, science, art, office, business (a) of healing by means of natural medicines (remedies) or supernatural medicines (charms); (b) of divining the unknown by consulting the shades of the deceased, or the genii, demons, who are spirits neither human nor divine ; (c) of inducing these human and non-human spirits to influence men and nature for human weal or woe. (2) The forces at work in healing, divining, and in the influence of spirits. (3) The objects (charms) which are supposed to establish and determine the connection between the spirits and the physical world.[68]

---

65 *Dicionário kimbundu-português, linguístico, botânico, histórico e corográfico. Seguido de um índice alfabético dos nomes próprios*, Assis Junior (1887- 1961).

66 Kimbánda. sub. (Ill) Pessoa que trata de doentes. Mágico; exorcista; necromante; bruxo.

67 Umbanda, sub (V) Bruxaria; magismo. I Arte ou maneira de encantar, de curar; kubanga- \ Produção de actos mágicos.

68 *Folk-Tales of Angola*, Héli Chatelain.

That the musical instruments were also named *macumba* is a sure fact; however, there is also the possibility that the transposition of the name happened from the opposite direction:

The word is of Bantu origin but of controversial etymology. [It may] refers to the Kimbundu macumba, plural of dikumba, 'padlock', 'lock', and in view of the "closing ceremonies of bodies" that take place in these rituals. However, the origin appears to be in the quicongo makumba, plural of kumba, 'prodigies', 'miraculous facts', linked to the cumba, 'sorcerer'.[69]

When the Macumba branched into the Umbanda and the Quimbanda, the original meaning of these words underwent important changes to suit the new needs.

## Umbanda versus Quimbanda

The emergence of *Quimbanda* is intimately linked to the creation of Umbanda in the first decades of the 20th century. The process of the creation of Umbanda, however, was not so straightforward as the later myth surrounding the figure of Zélio Fernandino de Moraes (1891– 1975) would have people believe.

Arthur Ramos (1903-1949), Brazilian psychiatrist, social psychologist, ethnologist, folklorist and  anthropologist, in his work from 1934 testified to the fluid use of the terms *umbanda* and *quimbanda* in the Macumbas of the Rio de Janeiro; there *umbanda* could mean a priest, a sorcerer, the art, the place where the macumba were performed, a "nation" or a spirit. *Quimbanda* also appear as a name for the ritual.[70]

---

69 *Enciclopédia Brasileira da Diáspora Africana*, Nei Lopes.

70 *O Negro Brasileiro*, Arthur Ramos.

The "myth" about Zélio says that when he was seventeen years old (1908) he was afflicted with a mysterious disease which could not be treated by the doctors nor exorcised by a priest. He was then taken to a meeting at the Spiritist Federation of Niterói, where the director invited him to sit at the table.

In the sequence, the young lad was possessed by a spirit who presented himself as the Caboclo Seven Crossroads. The *caboclo* (*caboclo* means a Native-Brazilian) then asked why the spirits of *caboclos* and *preto velhos* (Old Blacks) were not allowed to work at the Spiritist tables, and received the usual answer that these spirits were not evolved enough – Native Americans and Africans were considered people of a lower stage of evolution. The *caboclo* then proclaimed he would start a new religious movement where these spirits would have their chance to work helping the needy, and on the next day Zélio began to work in his house along with the spirit of an old black named Father Anthony, founding what would come to be known as the first Umbanda center or "tent," the "Spiritist Tent of Our Lady of Piety".

The first thing that catches our attention is the absence of any mention of the *exus* and *pombagiras* in the myth. According to the development of the story, Zélio was further instructed by the Caboclo Seven Crossroads to found seven new tents, which was done between 1918 and 1939.[71] Only the fifth, the Spiritist Tent Saint George, founded in 1935, worked with the *exus*, and was considered the first to do so (or so it was said). It is probably in this tent where "another revolution" inside the Umbanda happened,[72] when in 1940 the Caboclo Tupinamba ordered the table to be removed from the center of the room, giving space

---

71 http://pt.wikipedia.org/wiki/Umbanda
72 As ressignificações de Exu dentro da Umbanda, Lenny Francis Campos de Alvarenga.

QUEEN OF THE SEVEN CROSSROADS

for the *exus* and *pombagiras* to manifest after the *caboclos* and old blacks.[73]

As we see in the research of Vagner Gonçalves da Silva,[74] the myth of the founding of Umbanda which focused on the figure of Zélio is a very late elaboration created after the 1960's: there is no mention of it in the documentation of the associations and congresses organized by the Umbandists before that period, where Zélio is a respected but very secondary character. However, the myth is of interest to us for two reasons.

First, we should notice the similarities between what would have happened to Zélio and the *mahamba* spirits process. The *mahamba* spirits were originally considered to be *outsiders*: spirits from the forest or from other societies. The Caboclo of the Seven Crossroads was clearly an outsider when he manifested at the Spiritist meeting. The process of affliction to which he submitted Zélio to also very typical.

Second, we see the designation "of the Seven Crossroads" was already being used at the time; when interpellated the caboclo explained this designation saying that he used it "because for me there will be no closed paths". He also affirmed that in a previous life, before reincarnating as a Brazilian Indian, he was the Italian Jesuit missionary Gabriel Malagrida (1689 –1761), who was strangled and had his body burnt by the Inquisition under the accusation of heresy.[75] The declaration of the spirit (below), however, was historically inaccurate as Malagrida was accused of heresy and not witchcraft.

---

73 The last two paragraphs are borrowed from my paper "The Gnosis of the Devil".

74 *Caminhos da alma: memória afro-brasileira*, Vagner Gonçalves da Silva.

75 *Descomplicando os Guias de Umbanda*, Eliana Pacco.

What you see in me are remnants of an earlier existence. I was priest, my name was Gabriel Malagrida. Accused of witchcraft I was sacrificed at the stake of the Inquisition in Lisbon, in the year of 1761. But in my last physical existence God granted me the privilege of being born as a Brazilian caboclo.

Leaving all the dubious mythic narration aside, what the historical evidences point to is a diffuse process where Macumba was reinterpreted under Kardecist concepts, leaving aside the most preposterous elements that would be identified under the name of Quimbanda. These elements were intimately associated with the class of spirits identified as *exus* and *pombagiras*, spirits that contrary to the *caboclos* and old blacks could "do evil". Under the Kardecist ideas of spiritual evolution, however, these spirits ended up being reintegrated as long as they pledged to abandon the evil works and submit to the rule of the good spirits. The word Quimbanda then acquired a double meaning: when integrated into Umbanda it indicates the part of the ritual where these spirits manifest, but when isolated it is associated with black magic and evil works. The *exus* and *pombagiras* spirits that take part in the first are called "doctrinated" or "baptized"; the still "evil" *exus* and *pombagiras* outside the control of the Umbanda are called "pagan".

And Quimbanda with her pagan-exus? For Umbandist intellectuals, this would have to be excluded from the rituals; but this practice continues in the daily life of the terreiros, and even though there are some houses that consider themselves to be of Umbanda White Line, the great majority also practices Quimbanda. If it were possible to make divisions, we would say that Umbanda is divided into two (Umbanda/Quimbanda) and Quimbanda is also divided into two (the one of the baptized exus and the one of the pagan exus). But I believe that in reality, the field of Afro-Brazilian religions is very fluid, and there is certainly no well-defined boundary between the modalities discussed here (Umbanda, Quimbanda, Candomblé), given that the same terreiro can practice them, for example, the Umbanda on the Mondays, the Quimbanda on the Fridays, and hold Candomblé parties on commemorative dates. [...]At least not in the great majority of the terreiros, there is no such separation, since Quimbanda is inserted inside the Umbanda. But it is possible to generate a reasoning: Macumba is a religion present in the Afro-Brazilian religious field, including that researched by me, and is often confused with Umbanda. And it is possible to measure how close a terreiro can be, to the Macumba or to the Umbanda, through the analysis of Quimbanda: the stronger the role of the exu, the more close to the Macumba the terreiro is.[76]

---

76 *Cultos Híbridos no que é Afro-Brasileiro: Qual a Fronteira entre Umbanda, Quimbanda e Candomblé?*, Saulo Conde Fernandes.

# POMBAGIRA

◆

The most accepted etymology for "Pombagira" derives the word from Bombonjira or Bombagira, variations of Pambu Njila, the quimbundo deity from the north of Angola equivalent to the Eshu. Eshu is a key element in the functioning of the religious system of the Yoruba, in charge of transmitting requests and offerings from people to the orishas. He is a god of divination that translates the language of the deities to us and inspects the adequacy of the sacrifices and other religious performances, bringing punishment when necessary. He is "the wrath of God", but he is not a passive agent as he takes initiative to put to test the people that he will then judge and punish. In this aspect he is close to the figure of Satan in the Old Testament when he tempts God and then tests Job.

Eshu is directly connected to human sexuality and often was represented in Africa as a couple or even as female, which may have helped his transition to the Brazilian Pombagira; according to the testimony of the British Army officer and ethnographer Alfred Burdon Ellis (1852–1894), with his other name of Elegba he could manifest as a man or as woman in dreams and have sex with the sleepers, which led to Ellis associating him with the European incubi and succubi.[77] In fact, the phallic character of Eshu, his association, not just with sex, but also with magic, very early led to his identification with "l'esprit du mal, le Béelphégor des Moabites, le Priape des Latins, *Deus turpitudinis*, comme dit Origène".[78] Eshu's role as Lord of Sex and Magic matched well with

---

77 Ellis, A. B. *The Yoruba-Speaking Peoples of the Slave Coast of West Africa, Etc.* (Photomechanic Reprint of the Edition of 1894.). Anthropological Publications, 1966.

78 *La Côte des Esclaves et le Dahomey*, Abbé Pierre Bouche (1885).

the figure of the Devil and this helps to explain the iconography and attributes of the Brazilian *exus* and *pombagiras*. As it happened with the Bantu ancestors, the roles that associates Eshu with the image of Satan of Job also associates him with the idea that he could "do both good and evil". Again, here the concept of evil is not metaphysical like in Christianity but relates to the idea that the person did something wrong (not necessarily morally wrong, but perhaps ritualistically wrong) and Eshu is the one responsible for "making things right" – no matter what it costs.

The anthropologist and ethnologist Stefania Capone considered the Pombagira to be "a purely carioca creation",[79] "carioca" being a demonym referring the City of Rio de Janeiro. The earliest reference to the term which Capone found was in a newspaper from 1938, but the journalist João do Rio had already mentioned it in his book *As Religiões do Rio* published in 1904.

## The Multiplicity of Eshu

How did the orisha Eshu multiply into the extensive and ever-growing legions of *exus* and *pombagiras* from the Brazilian Quimbanda? We must know first that *multiplicity* is a key concept regarding Eshu. As he is the orisha of movement itself, the intermediary *par excellence*, the ruler of the ways and of the entrances, it follows that his presence is *everywhere*. That led to the concept that Eshu is somehow present with everyone all the time, so people started talking about the Eshu of each orisha, the Eshu of each person... The "personal Legba" in Africa was linked to a special image that should be destroyed after the death of its owner or "the door to the world of death would remain

---

79 Capone, Stefania. *A Busca Da Africa No candomblé: tradição e Poder No Brasil*. Pallas, 2018.

always open".[80] The personal Legbas of children and women were dependent on the Legba of the principal member of the family.[81] Variations and epithets of Eshu existed for the different places where he was propitiated, like crossroads, markets, doorways, etc. We have a good example in the excellent work of Ócha'ni Lele:

Elegguá: He is often portrayed as fate, a young child, and an old man. Elegguá is the messenger of all the orishas and the first and last to be honored in every ceremony performed. Without his goodwill, nothing in Santería may be done. In Ifá, it is said that there are 256 paths of Elegguá, one for each odu. Each of these paths is known as an Eshu and has its own specific name, such as Eshu Ayé, Eshu Bi, and Eshu Laroye. In ocha, there are 101 paths of Elegguá (each also known as Eshu). In many ilé ocha, when an initiate receives the warriors, he is told the name of Eshu that his Elegguá enshrines.[82]

Pierre Verger registered the connection between the idea of multiplicity of Eshu and the number 7 in Bahia: there would be 7, 21 or 21 X 21 Eshus. He also mentioned the existence of a cult of a feminine version called "Exu Vira".[83]

We have some signposts for this metamorphosis that we can organize and then try to connect the dots. First, we know that the identification of Eshu with the Devil was to a large extent absorbed by the African descendants themselves, which caused

---

80 Capone, Stefania. A Busca Da Africa No candomblé: tradição e Poder No Brasil. Pallas, 2018.

81 Ibid.

82 Sacrificial Ceremonies of Santería: A Complete Guide to the Rituals and Practices, Ócha'ni Lele.

83 Notas Sobre o Culto aos Orixás e Voduns na Bahia de Todos os Santos, Pierre Verger.

general aversion and reluctance towards the orisha. The concept that each orisha was attended by its specific *exu*, sometimes called "the slave of the orisha", gave rise to a misconception where the "individual" *exus* started to receive more and more independent characters and personalities. The American cultural anthropologist Ruth Landes (1908-1991), who researched the candombles of Bahia in 1938-1939, found this new dimension already well established:

> Eshu is a goblin-creature involved in evil magic. He does not possess the sternness ascribed to the great gods but is indispensable to cult practice. The people call him "devil" but more in the sense of servant than of demon. One priestess called him "slave" because he performs malicious errands in exchange for the offering of a few fractions of a cent, a little oil and sugar rum. [...] He is ready for service at any time, resting at the cross-roads. There are different types of Eshu but all are regarded in this ambivalent way. There is a sort of domesticated Eshu, often called "godfather", who is regarded both as guarding the home and as restraining his own evil self from entering the home in view of the regular offerings made to him. There are however "wild" Eshus ranging the highways and woods, especially at dawn, midday and midnight.[84]

We find here already many of the attributes of the *exus* and *pombagiras* from Umbanda and Quimbanda. The appellative "godfather" (Portuguese "compadre") is typical of the intimate and affectionate relationship between these entities and their followers. The position of the *exus* and *pombagiras* shrines at the

---

84 Landes, Ruth. "Fetish Worship in Brazil." *The Journal of American Folklore*, vol. 53, no. 210, 1940, p. 261., doi:10.2307/535786.

entrance of the houses indicate they act as guardians too. Landes' testimony helps us see that the hard separations proposed by earlier academics, like Verger, between Candomble, Macumba and Umbanda / Quimbanda never corresponded to the reality where the "ideal types" for these religious denominations never occur. Landes was much more keen than Verger and Bastide in her observations, did not allow herself to be fooled as they were:

[...] Eshu is employed secretly to arrange a rendezvous, to force a seduction, to disrupt or even mend a marriage. "Mothers" of the renowned fetish temples deny employing Eshu, indicating that they consider themselves above petty interests, but they all know what formulas to use with him privately. Inasmuch as the Catholic Church stigmatizes Eshu as diabolic, priestesses are constrained to favor the gods, which are identified with the great Catholic saints.[85]

Landes' assessment indicates that researchers like Verger and Bastide, even when becoming initiates themselves, were naive and were not caught up in what was going on behind the scenes. Landes' observation put the actual practices of the Candombles in Bahia much closer to the Macumbas in Rio de Janeiro than they would like to admit. It crumbles all the well written analyses that considered the Camdombles of Bahia representatives of a pure religion of Yoruba descent in opposition to the low and almost criminal Bantu manifestations of the Macumba Carioca.

---

85 Landes, Ruth. "Fetish Worship in Brazil." *The Journal of American Folklore*, vol. 53, no. 210, 1940, p. 261., doi:10.2307/535786.

# The Rise of Quimbanda

The associations of Umbanda were doing their best to distance themselves from Macumba; to have a good idea as to why, let's just mention that a newspaper reference from 1938 about a raid done by the Police against a center of Macumba, where they found a sign that offered the services of *exus* and *pombagiras* for the fee of seven-thousand réis and consultation with the same spirits for five-thousand. It happened in the same year that Zélio de Moraes moved his house of Umbanda from Niteroi to the center of Rio de Janeiro.

We can deduct the following process in the development of Macumba into Umbanda: *first*, we have the Bantu inspired ceremonies like the ones performed at the end of the 19th century by Juca Rosa with the "incorporation" (spirit possession) of entities of clearly African origin which would become the Old Blacks: Father Quibombo, Saint Zuza and Father Vencedor ("Victorious"). We also see here a proximity with the religious practice of the *Cabula* found in the neighboring state of Espírito Santo. There are several similarities between the Cabula and the Macumba,[86] one of them being that Juca Rosa had a ritualistic assistant called "cambondo" similar to the "cambono" from the Cabula – a word probably derived from the Kimbundu "kabanda", which was the person that assisted or even substituted for the Angolan kimbanda[87] in his practices.

*Second*, the Macumba in Rio de Janeiro began to appropriate spirits that were popular in other Afro-Brazilian religions. From the Cabula it took the Tatá Caveira and Tatá Veludo which would become important *exus*; from the Candomble of Caboclo

---

86 See *Cabula e Macumba*, Valdeli Carvalho da Costa.

87 *Dicionário kimbundu-português, linguístico, botânico, histórico e corográfico. Seguido de um índice alfabético dos nomes próprios*, Assis Junior (1887- 1961).

practiced in the North it took the *caboclos*, the original spirits of the land, and with the *exus* from the Candombles of Bahia the fundamental triad was complete.

In *third* place, in the first decades of the 20th century the spirits and practices of Macumba were mixed with Kardecist concepts and ideals to form Umbanda. In the struggles against religious persecution and in the search for social acceptance the *exus* were initially denied or hidden. Lines like the "Umbanda Branca" ("White Umbanda") still do not accept the *exus* and *pombagiras* in their works.

The process of acceptance of the *exus* and *pombagiras* developed in parallel with a change in the way these spirits were seen. According to testimonies from practitioners[88] around the 1950s the exus very rarely possessed the mediums and when it happened they were quickly dispatched. Sometimes they were allowed a brief time of possession to "clean" the energies after the work. The possessed mediums twisted, crawled on the floor, gave roars and laughter and licked on the floor the drink they paid to the spirit.

Curiously, it was the Kardecist ideas about spiritual evolution that allowed the image and cult of the *exus* and *pombagiras* to evolve. Initially the *exus* imported from the Candoble that Ruth Landes described were associated with the souls of dead suicides, criminals, people of perverted nature, and prostitutes. These wild and dangerous spirits should agree to work for the *Caboclos* and the Old Blacks, upgrading themselves from "pagan exus" to "baptized exus" that would no longer be used to work evil but only to perform good deeds in exchange for "light". Here Quimbanda began to indicate not just the work of evil sorcerers who would

---

88 Marques, Rodrigo. *Os outsiders do além: um estudo sobre a quimbanda e outras 'feitiçarias' afro-gaúchas.*

do anything for money, but a part of the Umbanda ritual where the exus would work *against* the magical attacks done against the house and its clients.

With the extension of the time and space given to the manifestation of the *exus* and *pombagiras* indicated in the event of 1940 in the Tent Saint George in Rio de Janeiro, the Quimbanda of Umbanda accelerated its emergence; practitioners began to talk about the "Crossed Line" where the temples performed rituals for the Orishas, *Caboclos* and Old Blacks *and* rituals for the *exus* and *pombagiras* on *separate* occasions. It is then that the figure of the *Exu de Alta*[89] appears. We can discern this in the trajectory of yalorixá Ieda de Ogum, considered to be one of the first "quimbandeiras" in the state of Rio Grande do Sul. In the 1960s she began to be possessed by the exu King of the Seven Crossroads who manifested in a very different fashion, with the refined behavior to be expected from someone who had noble origins in his previous life.

From this, the thing exploded. Testimonies from the practitioners in Rio Grande do Sul refer to the great popularity quickly achieved by these rituals of Quimbanda, overshadowing the rituals done with the *caboclos* and old blacks. The *exus* and *pombagiras*, elevated to the ranks of lords, with their kings and queens, could now begin to expand their realms into the entire world.

---

89 "Alta" means "high", in reference to "high society", but can be expanded here to mean a "higher evolution", and be associated with the idea of "High Magic".

# Yabás

In the evolution of the *pombagiras* of Quimbanda another source of inspiration helped to elevate their image – the feminine orishas. In Ruth Landes' work we already find a crucial mention of the "feminine exus" and their connection to one of the Yabas, the orisha Yansan:

> Every god appears to have one or more Eshu-lackeys doing the dirty-work for him; the warrior goddess Yansan has a "gang" of at least seven of the "wildest" and they are all female.[90]

Iansã ("Yansan"), originally Oya in Yoruba, is an orisha with characteristics that brings her very close to the *pombagira*: she is not just the deity of winds, lightning, and violent storms, but she rules in the market and at the gates of the cemetery – two places also connected to Eshu. She is considered to be the lady of the *eguns*, the spirits of the dead, a psychopomp who leads the souls of the dead to their destinations but who is also capable of raising them to do battle. She is a warrior Goddess that holds a sword or machete, and because of the sword and the lightning she was syncretized with Saint Barbara, who usually holds a sword in her images and is associated with lightning.

---

90 Landes, Ruth. "Fetish Worship in Brazil." *The Journal of American Folklore*, vol. 53, no. 210, 1940, p. 261., doi:10.2307/535786.

Saint Barbara, popular image.

QUEEN OF THE SEVEN CROSSROADS

In the Seven Lines division of Umbanda, she rules over the Line of the Souls. The verse "Iansã foi quem lhe deu força" ("Iansã was who gave her strength") appears in several *pontos cantados* for higher *pombagiras* like the Queen of the Crossroads and Maria Padilha.

Iansã emits vibrations to solve the most diverse problems, but that need a quick outcome. She is also invoked when there are spirits damaging a certain situation, ghosts and disembodied souls obsessors. The subjects with which she has greater affinity are those which concern sentimental problems, storms and tempests that destroy homes and crops, industries, etc. Iansã rules health problems related to the reproductive system of both sexes.[91]

The epithet *Yabá* was originally given only to the feminine orishas Oshun and Yemanja, but in Brazil it was extended and used for all the feminine deities originating from the Yoruba pantheon. It means "Mother Queen".

The great Oshun is the orisha of sweet water: rivers, lakes and waterfalls are her sacred places. She has rulership over fertility, sexuality, beauty, pleasure, and love; she is also related to matters of destiny and divination, and she is the Lady of Gold, so has power and precedence over matters of riches. But to us here it is important that in her aspect (path) of Oshun Ibu Ikole (Oshun the Vulture), she is considered to be Queen of Witches, an epithet also given to Yemoja Okutti.

It's no coincidence Oshun is also referred to as the queen of the witches: She is a teacher of both magic and mysticism. Oshun loves casting spells, especially those related to romance and seduction. She is the granter of

---

91 *Orixás na Umbanda*, Janaina Azevedo.

wishes and all of your heart's desires. When respected and properly invoked, Oshun holds the keys to love, success, prosperity, and pregnancy.[92]

Yemoja is the Queen of the Sea; we must first understand that in Banto language the word for cemetery and sea are the same, so in Brazil we say "The Great Calunga" to indicate the sea and the "The Small Calunga" to indicate the cemetery. The sea is, in fact, a great cemetery where the drowned from uncountable ages lie, and sometimes the Bantus believed that the dead had to cross the sea or even that they lived under it. Yemoja is also considered to be Queen of the Witches in her aspect/path of Yemoja Okutti, when she dances with a serpent around her arms.

Yemoja is the second wife of the greater orisha Oxala; the first is Nana. Nana is originally the female Supreme Being of the Fon Ewe people, and kept some of this original prestige when she became the first wife of Oxala and helped him to create humankind by giving him the fertile mud from which he modeled us. From this came her power over the dead who return to her; her daughter Iansã inherited her necromantic powers from her. She is powerful and very knowledgeable about magic.

We can see that the Yabas not only related directly to the *pombagiras* as having their own "gang" (as Ruth Landes said of Iansã) but they were a model where sexuality, witchcraft and necromancy already coexisted in the same figure, together with the idea of the "queen". As the concept of the "exu de alta" began to take hold, the relationship of the practitioners of Quimbanda with their *exus* and *pombagiras* came closer to the worship previously given to the orishas; today that is how many

---

92 Mesa, Valerie. "How to Invoke Oshun, the Yoruba Goddess of Sensuality and Prosperity." Vice, 20 Apr. 2018, https://broadly.vice.com/en_us/article/3kjepv/how-to-invoke-oshun-yoruba-goddess-orisha.

quimbandeiros approach the higher entities who receive the epithets of Kings and Queens.

## Rosa Caveira

The *pombagiras* then inherited different inspirations that often disagree between themselves. From one side the reinterpretation of the entities described by Ruth Landes under a Kardecist point of view considered the *exus* and *pombagiras* to be the souls of criminals, suicides and prostitutes in a very low degree of evolution; from the African side, however, these entities were associated with the great orisha Eshu and with the royal Yabás, full of beauty and magic.

The conciliation between these extremes has been facilitated through the creation of myths; as the *pombagiras* began to multiply as more and more mediums began to work regularly with them, so many different stories were created – often narrated by the entities themselves. Some of these tales, like the one ascribed to the spirit of Maria Navalha ("Razor Mary"), talk indeed about women forced into prostitution, but other differing tales began to be told to accommodate different spirits, like the myth of Rosa Caveira ("Skull Rose"), the first *pombagira* with whom I had a close relationship.

The myth of Rosa Caveira is a very good example of the syncretism that still works toward creating more complex forms of Quimbanda. She is a *pombagira* whose origins in the tale lie in the Orient, where she was born as the seventh daughter of a powerful sorceress who died giving birth to her. As she inherited the powers from her mother, and learned to use them directly from the spirit of the deceased woman at her grave, she was envied by her six sisters who in the end succeeded in killing her.

Before her death, she was trained by her father in the use of swords and daggers, and by an old sage in the craft of necromancy. Her sisters contracted a criminal sorcerer who killed her and had her spirit imprisoned by keeping her skull. The necromantic sage who educated her released her spirit, who then killed and enslaved the souls of the sorcerer and her six sisters, keeping them forever under her control.

The story about the previous life of a *pombagira* usually has aetiological motives that explain her areas of operation and her iconography. The image of Rosa Caveira shows a woman in a robe with half of her face in the shape of a skull, or half or her body in the shape of a skeleton, usually holding a skull or a rose or a knife in her hands. From this then it is clear that her line of work involves necromancy and revenge; she is not the most suitable therefore for works of love. She is said to be very loyal and protective of her followers.

# THE BOOKS OF QUIMBANDA

The historical process we described so far should not be understood as a clear and straightforward development; Umbanda and Quimbanda even today reveal themselves as very variable fields and we can find divergent examples of conduct and interpretation that in fact are rooted in the motley crew array of Macumba's original centers.

For instance, contradicting the experience of many terreiros of Umbanda (where the *exus* incorporated in the savage and degraded fashion described as late as the 1960's), we have a description of an Exu's incorporation in the first book of Umbanda published in 1925,[93] in which the Exu talks normally with the audience whilst walking over embers and performing magical deeds. In this fundamental work the division between the White Line, with the *caboclos* and the "blacks", in opposition to the Black Line of the *exus* is made very clear. The place to work with the *exus* is the crossroad and they are justly called "people of the Crossroad".

> Such entities are proud of their power; they are often irritable and vindictive, but when they want to please a friend of the Earth, they go to great lengths to satisfy him. Their struggles in space, for earth's matters, have the terrible greatness of battles and tragedies. This magic exerts its daily disturbing influence over the existence, in Rio de Janeiro. Hundreds of people of all classes, poor and rich, large and small, for reasons of love, for reasons of hatred, for reasons of interest, resort to their sorcery.

---

93 *O Espiritismo, a Magia e as Sete Linhas de Umbanda*, Leal de Souza.

Politicians were and continue to be some of its best and most frequent clients.[94]

After Leal de Souza comes the controversial work of Aluízio Fontenelle, who in the 1950's published three books of Umbanda. Fontenelle goes backwards in the process of humanization of the *exus* and returns to the diabolical vision defended by the first missionaries. He identifies Exu with Lucifer and the Universal Magical Agent from Eliphas Levi's books and names him and his "people" as the main culprits in the drama of the Genesis – all this substantiated by references to the "original" Bible that he affirms was written in the Hindu language "Palli" 15,000 years ago.

Fontenelle closely follows Souza's distinction between Umbanda ("White Magic or middle spiritism") and Quimbanda ("Black magic or low Spiritism"), considering Kardecism as superior to them and "scientific".[95]

In the Umbanda one does not practice evil, whereas in the Quimbanda, only revenge is conceived, and its works of black magic, only intend to harm this or those who oppose their interests.[96]

If we try to make sense of Fontenelle's ideas, it seems that he tries to bring together the diabolical views with the evolutionary scheme from Kardecism by putting the "lower or backward spirits" that "comprises the caste of bad elements, ignorant, sufferers, obsessors" under the power of the original People of Exu. The evil dead are "forced by a law of justice" to inhabit the kingdom

---

94 *O Espiritismo, a Magia e as Sete Linhas de Umbanda*, Leal de Souza.

95 *O Espiritismo no Conceito das Religiões e a Lei de Umbanda*, Aluizio Fontenelle.

96 Ibid.

of darkness, the natural place of "all the phalanxes of evil under the dominion and direction of Exu-King Lucifer".[97]

Fontenelle was forced to compromise because, as we can glimpse in his writings, a quarter of a century after Souza´s publication the Exus had already established a firm hold in the works of Umbanda:

Just as there are the good spirits, there are also the bad ones, and in order to command them, the practitioners of Umbanda believe in the existence of the dark spirits, which with the denomination of "EXUS" take care of the cleaning of the terreiros, and are considered the servants of the Greater Orishas.[98]

The phalanxes of exus when employed in Quimbanda follow their evil inclinations and "just do evil things"; but when called to work in Umbanda "they are forced [...] to undo the evil that perhaps they did to this or that person".[99] The *exus* are again considered to be "servants" or "slaves" of the Orishas and are forced by the deities to work for humans. More than that, they also recovered to some extent the role of intermediaries and punishers that belonged to their Orisha of inspiration:

The EXUS are diabolical spirits, considered as servants or slaves of the *Orishas*, serving as intermediaries between the *Lesser Orishas* and man. These are the entities that are responsible to punish the sons of the faith when they

---

97 A *Umbanda Através dos Séculos*, Aluízio Fontenelle.

98 *Espiritismo no Conceito das Religiões e a Lei de Umbanda*, Aluizio Fontenelle.

99 Ibid.

err, as to the *Orishas* is not given the right to punish and even less they are charged with the practice of evil.[100]

In Fontelle we also see two important elements we mentioned when tracing the development of Quimbanda: (1) the Exus are the guardians of the center of Umbanda, having a "tronqueira" (a small place at the front of the house where their images are housed) where they are always "saluted" before any work starts; and (2) the hierarchy of the *exus* that allowed the concept of the "exu de alta" to appear. In fact, the King of the Seven Crossroads that began to incorporate in the yalorixá Ieda de Ogum in the 1960's is already mentioned in the two hierarchical descriptions given by Fontenelle:

Let us therefore leave Quimbanda aside, and let us speak again of the spiritual entity of evil that is EXU, which, in any way as it is seen, does not fail to render its innumerable benefits as well. The EXU, greatest symbol of black magic, also has its cortege of chiefs, and the maioral[101] is known as said by: SATANAZ or LUCIFER.

Possessing a large army, they are invoked both in the Umbanda and in the Quimbanda, according to the phalanges or legions to which they belong, with the following denominations:

Exu-Rei (Lucifer, Satanas, Diabo, etc.)
Exu of 7 Crossroads
Exu Caveira
Exu Tiriri
Exu of Wind (or of the 7 wind storms)

---

100 A *Umbanda Através dos Séculos*, Aluízio Fontenelle.
101 "The maioral", literally "the greatest", is an epithet for the Devil already attested to in confessions from the Portuguese Inquisition.

Exu of the 7 Keys
Exu Tranca-Rua ("Lock-Street")
*Exu Pomba-Gira (woman of 7 exus)*
Exu Maré ("Tide")
Exu of the Rivers
Exu of the Woods[102]

The Exu of 7 Crossroads appears here as the second in the hierarchical arrangement. This Exu and the Exu Tranca-Rua are the only ones to have a *ponto cantado* and a *ponto riscado* mentioned in the book (there is also a *ponto cantado* addressing the collective of exus):

| | |
|---|---|
| O meu senhor das armas, | My lord of the guns, |
| Dize que eu não vale nada | Says I am worthless |
| Oia lá que eu é Exu, | Look there that I am Exu |
| Rei das 7 Encruzilhadas. | King of 7 Crossroads. |

In Souza's book from 1925 we already find a division of Umbanda into "7 Lines", each one headed by an Orisha (Oxalá); Ogum; Euxoce (Oxóssi); Xangô; Nha-San (Iansã); Amanjar (Iemanjá) with the exception of the seventh, the Line of Saints or Line of the Souls that "is transverse, and maintains its unity through the others".[103] Fontenelle gives the 7 Lines as headed by Oxalá/Jesus Christ; Iemanjá/Virgin Mary; Saint

John Baptist (Line of the Orient or of Magic); Oxoce/Saint Sebastian; Xango/ Saint Jerome; Ogum/Saint George; Saint Cyprian (African Line). Each line in turn is divided by Fontenelle into 7 Legions,

---

102 O *Espiritismo no Conceito das Religiões e a Lei de Umbanda*, Aluizio Fontenelle.

103 O *Espiritismo, a Magia e as Sete Linhas de Umbanda*, Leal de Souza.

with the exception of the Line of Oxalá/Jesus Christ for which he mentions only one Legion of Saints. More importantly for us, however, is that Fontenelle also provides the list of the 7 Lines of Quimbanda (according to "some authors of books about Umbanda and Quimbanda"[104]):

$1^a$ – *Line of the Souls – headed by Omulu*
$2^a$ – *Line of the Skulls – headed by João Caveira ("John Skull")*
$3^a$ – *Line of Nago – headed by Gerêrê (people of Ganga)*
$4^a$ – *Line of Malei – headed by Exu-rei ("Exu-king") (people of Exu)*
$5^a$ – *Line of Mossurubi – headed by Caminaloá (African savages – Zulus, cafres, etc)*
$6^a$ – *Line of Caboclos Quimbandeiros – headed by Black Panther (American savages from north and south)*
$7^a$ – *Mixed Line – headed by Exu da Campina ("Exu of the Plain") or Exu of the Rivers (spirits from many races)*[105]

The division in Lines is important for us because it precedes the later division of Quimbanda into Kingdoms; the emphasis given by Fontenelle to Omulu/Saint Lazarus as Owner and Lord of the Cemeteries is also important because it established the distinction between the Crossroads and the Cemeteries that will be the most fundamental in the later system of Kingdoms of Quimbanda.

---

104 He is referring to Lourenço Braga's book from 1942, *Umbanda (Magia Branca) e Quimbanda (Magia Negra)*, where we have for the first time the 7x7 subdivisions of the Lines and also the 7 Lines of Quimbanda.

105 *O Espiritismo no Conceito das Religiões e a Lei de Umbanda*, Aluizio Fontenelle.

Known in the Umbanda as much as in the Quimbanda, Saint Lazarus, whose name in the Nago language is called OMULU or UMULUM, is the spiritual chief of the *"Line of the Souls"*, yet more known as Owner and Lord of the Cemeteries.[106]

Omulu, from the Yoruba *Obalúayé*, is the deity of smallpox that rules over other infectious diseases as well; that makes him the "Wrath of the Supreme God" as much as the supreme healer. Fontenelle says Omulu is only part of the Quimbanda because the Line of the Souls "belongs integrally to it", but when the intervention and protection of Omulu is necessary, the Line of the Souls "is invited to participate in the works of magic in the Law of Umbanda".[107]

In his other book, Fontenelle gives a more detailed description of the hierarchies of Quimbanda; in fact, he gives *two* charts that seem to emphasize the distinction between the Cemetery and the Crossroad. In an excerpt he apparently puts Omulu under the rule of the Maioral, which is a bit contradictory as he also said that "although the Quimbandistas have great predilection for this saint, this does not mean that Saint Lazarus commands one legion of evil spirits; on the contrary, this entity is considered as one of the strongest 'orishas' from the diverse spiritual levels".[108]

---

106 *O Espiritismo no Conceito das Religiões e a Lei de Umbanda*, Aluizio Fontenelle.

107 Ibid.

108 Ibid.

Being part of the phalanges of evil, there are integrating the "KINGDOM OF ODUM", 7 lines of Exus, which, directed by the Magical Agent "OMULU" or "OMULUM", the one entrusted by the Maioral to direct all the people working in the cemeteries. Some Umbandas and even the Quimbanda, usually make believe that this entity of evil is St. Lazarus; however, the true Omulum entity is the "GOD OF THE PLAGUE", as it has always been known through countless religions, and especially in the true Umbanda.[109]

The contradiction seems to reside in the identification Fontenelle makes in one book between Omulu and Saint Lazarus which he then denies in the other. Here Fontenelle also gives us a division between the *Kingdom of Obatalá* and the *Kingdom of Odum* that is in fact the description of the hierarchies of Umbanda and Quimbanda – another important clue to us. The two charts he gives to the Kingdom of Odum are introduced in the following excerpt:

We now see the division of the 2nd part, in which is conceived in the Esoteric and Initiatic Umbanda, the "KINGDOM OF ODUM" or of Earth. The following chart shows us the "reign of the PEOPLE OF EXU", in which LUCIFER, the Maioral, commands its seven lines of Agents of Evil, composed of 49 EXUS chiefs. These, in turn, are the heads of the phalanges of Exus, as in the division of THE KINGDOM OF OBATALA the ORIXAS are also the main chiefs.[110]

---

109 A *Umbanda Através dos Séculos*, Aluízio Fontenelle.
110 A *Umbanda Através dos Séculos*, Aluízio Fontenelle.

QUEEN OF THE SEVEN CROSSROADS

I really cannot see the 7 Lines in these charts; however, we have two important things to note in them.

**First**, the majority of the exus are masculine, with the one single exception being the Exu Pomba-Gira Woman of 7 Exus that I highlighted in the first hierarchical list on page 89. We see that at this stage "Pomba-Gira" seems to be a *name* of an entity and not a *category* of entities.

**Second**, in the charts Fontenelle makes the association between several *exus* and the demons from the French *Grimorium Verum*, a magical workbook published in the 18th century. That association would become as influential as it was controversial, being severely criticized by the people that endeavor to separate the image of the orisha Eshu from its syncretism with the Devil.

There is no clear harmonization between the charts and the 7 Lines, and the preeminent position of the Exu-King of the Seven Crossroads in the first list seems to be misplaced in the chart; he is equated with "Aschtaroth", one of the Three Chiefs from the *Grimorium Verum*, and it makes no sense that the minor demon "Agalieraps" is put over him. The confusion came from a misunderstanding on Fontenelle's part about the hierarchy described in the grimoire: each one of the Three Chiefs have two demons directly under his command, but the two demons under the direct command of Lucifer (Agaliarept and Satanachia) *are not* above Beelzebuth and Astaroth.

# ORGANOGRAMA DAS FALANGES DO
# POVO DE EXU

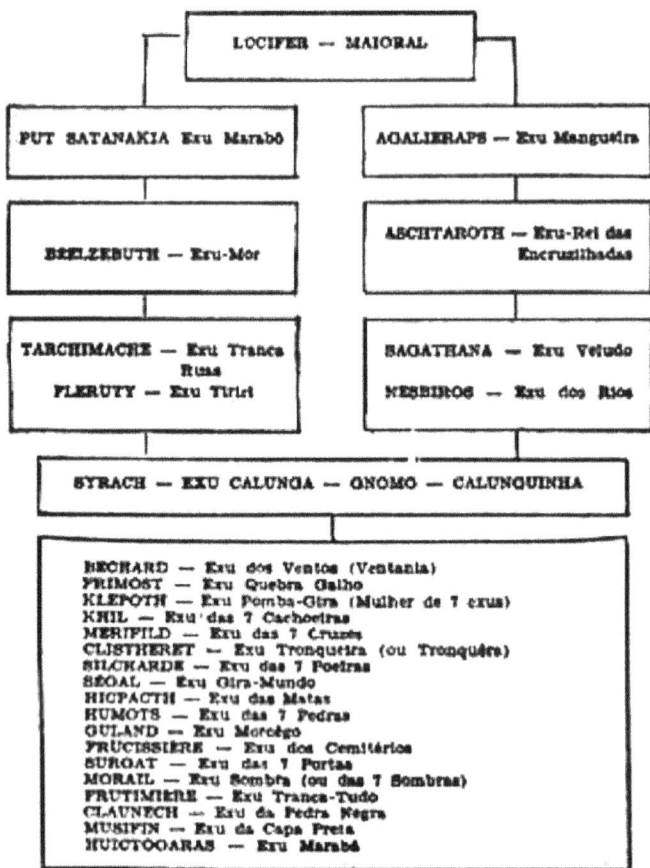

First chart, showing the hierarchy directly under the
command of the Maioral Lucifer

**ORGANOGRAMA DAS FALANGES DE EXUS QUE TRABALHAM SOB AS ORDENS DE OMULU (ou OMULUM)**

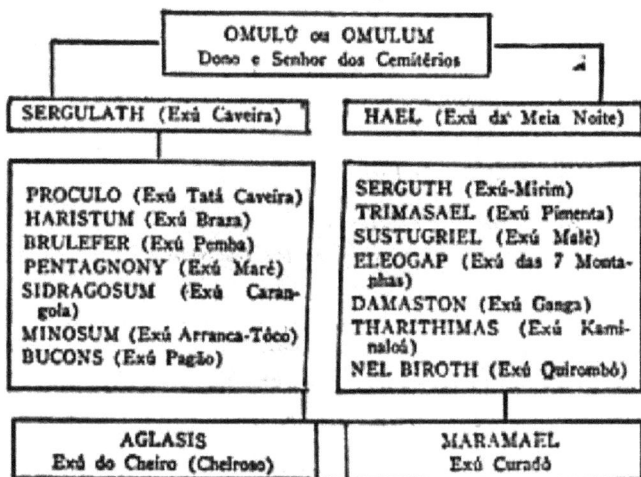

```
                ┌─────────────────────────────────┐
                │      OMULÚ ou OMULUM             │
        ┌───────│  Dono e Senhor dos Cemitérios   │────────┐
        │       └─────────────────────────────────┘        │
  ┌──────────────────────────┐       ┌──────────────────────────┐
  │ SERGULATH (Exú Caveira)  │       │ HAEL (Exú da Meia Noite) │
  └──────────────────────────┘       └──────────────────────────┘
```

| PROCULO (Exú Tatá Caveira) HARISTUM (Exú Braza) BRULEFER (Exú Pemba) PENTAGNONY (Exú Maré) SIDRAGOSUM (Exú Carangola) MINOSUM (Exú Arranca-Tôco) BUCONS (Exú Pagão) | SERGUTH (Exú-Mirim) TRIMASAEL (Exú Pimenta) SUSTUGRIEL (Exú Malé) ELEOGAP (Exú das 7 Montanhas) DAMASTON (Exú Ganga) THARITHIMAS (Exú Kaminaloá) NEL BIROTH (Exú Quirombó) |

| AGLASIS Exú do Cheiro (Cheiroso) | MARAMAEL Exú Curadô |

Second chart, showing the hierarchy of all the people working in the cemeteries entrusted to Omulu by the Maioral to direct.

# The Beautiful Angel

There are some doubts about the order and dates in which Aluizio Fontenelle's books were published during the 50's. He dedicated one of them exclusively to the subject of Quimbanda, the book entitled *Exu* with a second edition dated 1954. The fifth edition of *Umbanda Através dos Séculos* does not have a date but provides dates for his birth and death as 1913-1952. The same obituary is repeated in the third edition of *Espiritismo no Conceito das Religiões e a Lei de Umbanda*, also without a date of publishing.

Fortunately, we have some internal indications in the *Exu* from 1954 that clarify the matter; in this book Fontenelle says he had "recently published" the *Espiritismo no Conceito das Religiões e a Lei de Umbanda* and he speaks of the *Umbanda Através dos Séculos* as a work still to be published.[111] That clarifies his position regarding Omulu: in the first book he still identifies Omulu as the "name in the Nago language" for Saint Lazarus, but in the *Exu* he already distinguishes between the two.[112] In *Exu*, Omulu is "the entity of evil responsible for looking after the bodies deposited in the cemeteries" and he is in fact "Lucifer himself in another modality of work" or "in another outfit as it is usual to say in the giras[113] of Umbanda". This "other outfit" is described as "the form of a cadaver wrapped in a shroud".

---

111 Renato Guimarães on the site devoted to the history of Umbanda, Registros de Umbanda, gives these publication dates: 1950 – A *Umbanda através dos séculos*; 1951 – *Exu*; 1952 – O *Espiritismo no conceito das religiões e a lei de Umbanda*. This order does not agree with the internal testimony we find in Exu.

112 In *Exu* Fontenelle presents a *ponto riscado* for Omulu like the one we find in the first book (printed here), but without the name of Saint Lazarus on it.

113 *Gira* is the name of the meetings, probably derived from the name given in the Cabula for its ceremonies, *enjira*.

In *Exu* Fontenelle boldly states that "Umbanda was born from Quimbanda" because "Umbanda was created in the Higher Astral to fight the Quimbanda". We must observe that Fontenelle was part of the "whitening" party of Umbanda which tried to deny as much as possible its African origins. What they were then calling "Quimbanda" was in truth the Macumba of African origins from which they took the foundations for their new religion.

Always creative, in this work Fontenelle now explains the meaning of the word "exu" according to the "language of the spirits" called "Ijudice", spoken by God himself. The original word would have been "exud", meaning "traitor people", and was given to Lucifer, "the beautiful angel", and his followers. With time the word suffered modifications until it became "in the original Palli" the word "exu", meaning "the peoples". The fallen angels were exiled to the Island of Ceylon on the opposite side of Eden. The proximity led to the original sin and the expulsion of Adam and Eve.

This is how Fontenelle introduces the Devil of the Quimbanda:

*PONTO DO MAIORAL*

## THE HIGHEST ENTITY OF EVIL
## LUCIFER THE BEAUTIFUL ANGEL

The Highest Entity, is denominated "MAIORAL", having still other denominations, such as: Lucifer, Devil, Satanaz, Capeta, Tinhoso, etc., etc., being in the Umbandas better known with the name of "EXU-REI". He presents himself as a figure of high knowledge, treating us with a great elevation of sociability, promising us this world and the other, demanding only that by us he be treated as: MAJESTY. Rarely does he come to a terreiro, preferring only to approach the places where it is professed high studies of ASTRAL MAGIC, so that by the powers he is imbued with, and using a very special strategy, he seeks to shake or attract those who consider themselves porters of FAITH and, not infrequently, he prevails, because he can produce wonders immediately.

This is a perfect model for the "exus de alta", and Fontenelle speaks as if incorporations by the Maioral, although rare, *were already known*.

In *Exu* Fontenelle keeps the associations with the demons from the *Grimorium Verum*, according to which "Klepoth is the true name of *Exu Pomba-Gira*, the woman of 7 Exus". He gives the following description of the Exu Pomba-Gira:

POMBA GIRA takes care of revenge, pacting with female witches against their enemies. All the work inherent to love affairs, in which the woman feels harmed, or intends to make any union, are delivered to POMBA GIRA, and their results are in fact surprising, because this entity possess a great power. There is no Quimbandeiro, sorcerer or initiated in Magic, who does not know perfectly the

performance of the Exu Pomba-Gira, in the hierarchical
scale of the phalanges of the Power of Evil.

*Caracteres Kabalísticos de Exu Pomba Gira*

# THE QUEEN OF THE SEVEN CROSSROADS

—————— ❖ ——————

I am aware of two different myths regarding the Queen of the Seven Crossroads. The first makes her the soul of the Queen of Sheba and identifies King Solomon's soul with the King of the Seven Crossroads. The tale says that the true name of the Queen of Sheba was Samantha and that no woman loved Solomon more than she did. Their love was unfulfilled due to the prejudices of the Jewish court against her Ethiopic origin, and only after her death did Solomon recognized the mistake he had made. After his death they met again in the Astral Plane and began to work together to help the living fight against astral enemies.

The second tale is more elaborate, and speaks about an unnamed beautiful courtesan who married a king of France. She became the regent of the country after his untimely death, but due to the fact that she did not bear him children she was forced into a new marriage with a neighboring king who poisoned her after the marriage. Due to her faults, her soul got lost in the dark regions of the Astral World, until her first husband, now known as the Lord of the Crossroads, found and rescued her. Together they began to help the living and fight against astral enemies, and their many good deeds led them to be elevated by the Exu Belo ("The Beautiful Exu", Lucifer) to the ranks of King and Queen of the Seven Crossroads. When her second husband died in battle his soul was brought before her and forced to serve her for the rest of eternity.

These tales are completely of a mythical character; none of the forty-nine queens of France fit the description, and the character of the Queen of Sheba is considered to be a legend.

There are a few important notes to be made after these tales. *First*, we are very far from the demonic Pomba-Gira from

Fontenelle's book and completely inside the Kardecist view of penitent souls rescuing their karma through service. *Second*, the King and the Queen of the Seven Crossroads are perfect representatives of the "baptized exus" and "exus de alta" who are committed to doing only good actions. *Third*, Lucifer is not the evil and tricky entity described by Fontenelle but instead elevates the couple in recognition for their good deeds. *Fourth*, the role of the good *exus* as champions against "astral enemies" is strongly emphasized. The idea that the *exus* participate in astral battles was already present in Souza's book in a very interesting narrative about the astral ramifications of the Constitutionalist Revolution of 1932.

> During the Sao Paulo revolution, these hordes of space fought furious fights, hurling themselves at each other. Those who moved by the Paulistas came up against those that were put into action in favor of the dictatorship and these invisible clashes in the planes that our senses do not reach, certainly exceeded the fights in the material plane. Over the enraged disagreement of the so-called black legions, hovered the phalanges of the White Line of Umbanda and the good and superior spirits of all the nuclei of our cycle, raising fluidic defensive walls so that the rulers of Sao Paulo and Rio were not affected by the disturbance, and in the fullness of their faculties, measuring the extent of the misfortune, could understand the need to negotiate and conclude the peace. In these days of the civil war, the Umbanda White Line terreiros had a singular aspect: they were full of afflicted families, and almost deserted of protectors, because their phalanxes were all in the field of military operations, endeavoring to mitigate the brutality of armed discord ...[114]

---

114 *O Espiritismo, a Magia e as Sete Linhas de Umbanda*, Leal de Souza.

# The Kingdoms of Quimbanda

We saw that in Fontenelle's time a fundamental division was already becoming clear between the Cemeteries and the Crossroads. The Lines division of Quimbanda emphasized a classification of spirits according to *kind* or *place of origin*, but at some (still undetermined) moment a different arrangement evolved. Fontenelle already talked about the *Kingdom of Obatalá* and the *Kingdom of Odum* that divided the spirits between the good Umbanda and the evil Quimbanda, but then the Quimbanda and its spirits started to be seen in a better light and a division of Kingdoms focused on *places* emerged: Kingdom of Crossroads, Kingdom of the Cruzeiros,[115] Kingdom of the Woods, Kingdom of the Small Kalunga (cemeteries), Kingdom of Souls, Kingdom of the Lira and Kingdom of the Great Kalunga (Sea).

The concept of kingdom here refers to places of power where specific astral vibrations manifest strongly, thus allowing certain entities to manifest with more force. These entities are not necessarily bound to these places, but it is there that the connection with one of the realms can better happen. For instance, the spirits from the Kingdom of Souls, whose function is to help the souls at the moment of death, are more present in the places where this transition happens, from the last breath to the burial of the corpse: hospitals, morgues, funerary chapels. Once the funeral gets into the cemetery, if the soul still clings to the dead body, it enters into the Kingdom of the Small Kalunga, where it can become imprisoned. These souls of the dead, called *kiumbas*, can be forced to work for the *exus* of the Kingdom of the Small Kalunga or can be co-opted to serve a quimbandeiro.

---

115 The "cruzeiro" is the great cross at the center of the cemetery, often being the founding cross, the first cross to be erected.

The *cruzeiro*, the large founding cross usually at the center of the cemetery, also known as Cross of the Souls, is considered to be a gateway between the different planes of existence, and because of that it is believed that the spirits from the Kingdom of the Cruzeiros can also be contacted at liminal places like doors and gates. The notion of *cemetery* can be extended to the ocean, as we already saw, and the spirits from the Kingdom of the Great Kalunga are often the souls of the drowned; the same can be said of the Kingdom of the Woods.

The Kingdom of the Lira is associated with places of prostitution: motels, bohemia, bars, cabarets; with music, the arts, etc., so their works are much less necromantic and related to death than the others. Spirits from this kingdom are connected to music, dance, etc.

The Kingdom of Crossroads is usually the first in the kingdom lists we find in books. It is in fact the most close to the original concept of the orisha Eshu, who is not directly related to the mysteries of death. We saw that in the initial descriptions of Quimbanda another orisha, Omulu, was associated with the cemeteries. The Kingdom of Crossroads deals in the opening and closing of the ways, in the circulation of energies, communication and travels – attributions inherited from Eshu.

It seems that the "primary" Kingdom of Quimbanda was then the Crossroads; as we saw, there was a King of the Crossroads even before the division of kingdoms appeared. The addition of the Cemetery did not come as an inheritance from the original orisha Eshu, but evolved from the important role of the dead in the Bantu religion that was increased with the syncretism between Macumba and Kardecism. To this we have to add the Catholic influence: the Devotion to the Blessed Purgatory Souls is most likely the inspiration for the creation of the Line of the Souls. Catholics had a popular tradition of praying for the Souls in Purgatory, especially at Mondays, and the visit to the cemetery to pray for the dead is not just popular and traditional, it is part of official Church regulations:

## COEMETERII VISITATIO
### Visit to a Cemetery

*An indulgence, applicable only to the Souls in Purgatory, is granted to the faithful, who devoutly visit a cemetery and pray, even if only mentally, for the departed. The indulgence is plenary each day from the 1st to the 8th of November; on other days of the year it is partial.*[116]

## COEMETERII VETERUM CHRISTIANORUM
### SEU 'CATACUMBAE' VISITATIO
### Visit to an early Christian Cemetery or 'catacomb'

*A partial indulgence is granted to the faithful, who devoutly visit one of the early Christian cemeteries or "catacombs."*[117]

The Catholic orthodoxy sees the Souls in Purgatory as in need of our help, but denies them any power of intervention in our world or in our lives. Here is where the Portuguese *Book of Saint Cyprian* deviates and helped to create all the practices in Umbanda and Quimbanda where the souls in Purgatory and those imprisoned in their graves are beguiled or forced to provide magical services. Although the idea that the soul could be imprisoned in the grave is not orthodox, from examples as in the trial of the demonic nun Madalena de la Cruz in the 16th century we see that it could often go unchallenged.

---

116 Apostolica, Paenitentiaria. *Enchiridion of Indulgences: Norms and Grants.* Catholic Book Publishing, 1969.

117 Ibid.

The spirits of each realm are further divided into *legions* or *peoples*, a division closer to the original Line system; in the Kingdom of Crossroads we have:

Legion or People of the Crossroads of Street
Legion or People of the Crossroads of the Lira
Legion or People of the Crossroads of the Lomba[118]
Legion or People of the Crossroads of the Rails
Legion or People of the Crossroads of the Forest
Legion or People of the Crossroads of the Kalunga
Legion or People of the Crossroads of the Square
Legion or People of the Crossroads of the Space
Legion or People of the Crossroads of the Beach

From this, we see that the influence of the *exus* was extended to other places, some derived from the Line of Umbanda, or Line of the Orishas: the Beach that belongs to Iemanjá, and the Forest of Oxoce; places like the Street and the Square were already associated with Eshu, and the Rails can be seen as a modern equivalent of the Streets and Roads. The "Lira" is usually associated with the musical instrument lyre[119] (Greek: λύρα, *lýra*) with which Orpheus charmed the god of the Underworld Hades to retrieve his dead wife – a similar feat was also tried in vain by a kimbanda, as we saw.

I was very fortunate to find what seems to be the origins of the Kingdom of the Lira; we have a direct line of descent from

---

118 The top of a hill.

119 Sometimes people refer the "Lira" to a place, district, or city in Angola – this never existed. There is a city and district of Lira, however, in Uganda, where it was "the chief town and administrative headquarters of Lango District during the colonial period" (*Historical Dictionary of Uganda* by, M. Louise.). I do not see how the Kingdom of Lira of Quimbanda could be connected to it.

QUEEN OF THE SEVEN CROSSROADS

the Povo da Lira (People of the Lyre) or Turma da Lira (Gang of the Lyre) that roamed the center of Rio de Janeiro in the first decades of the 20th century, and to that we should add the great popularity that Orpheus (and the lyre by extension) enjoyed in Rio de Janeiro from the 1950's to the 1970's.

We know that the expression "people of..." is typical of the Quimbanda, so we have the People of the Street, the People of the Crossroads, etc. In the first decades of the 20th century in the same Rio de Janeiro where the Umbanda and the Quimbanda emerged, we had the People of the Lyre, a loose association of "capoeiras serenatistas", people who were adepts of the Capoeira, a "dancelike martial art of Brazil, performed to the accompaniment of call-and-response choral singing and percussive instrumental music",[120] and of the *serenatas* (serenades), romantic music of Italian origin usually played to a woman under a window. Both activities were a livelihood for their adepts; the *capoeiras* have worked for politicians as bodyguards since the end of the 19th century with pivotal roles in the elections.

Both activities were performed on the streets, which also helped to identify these kinds of people with the *exus* and *pombagiras*, the souls of marginalized people whose activities (like prostitution) mostly happened in the streets. In fact, the People of the Lyre in the first decades of the 20th century stood up bravely against the constrictions of the elitist social order, which earned them the epithet of "The Invincible People of the Lyre".

If the practice of capoeiragem was prohibited by law, and the formation of groups promoting singing, drumming or equivalent was inhibited by coercive police action, the existence of the "gang or people of the lyre" already represented a challenge factor to the republican order.[121]

---

120 Capoeira, *Encyclopaedia Britannica*.

121 Da *"Turma Da Lira" ao Cafajeste: A Sobrevivência da Capoeira no Rio*

The bohemian "valentes",[122] "bambas"[123] or "cafajestes"[124] that were part of this group are the direct predecessors of the "malandros"[125] that were also enshrined in Umbanda and Quimbanda.

The story of Orpheus became very popular in Brazil in the 1950's:[126] the poet and politician Jorge de Lima published the poetic book *Invenção de Orfeu* in 1952; the Modernist poet Murilo Monteiro Mendes published four poems inspired by the Thracian hero during this period and, most importantly, a musical stage play by Brazilian musicians Vinicius de Moraes and Antônio Carlos Jobim, *Orfeu da Conceição*, premiered in 1956 and was filmed in Rio de Janeiro by film director and French writer Marcel Camus in 1959. If we note that the Kingdoms of Quimbanda were not mentioned in Fontenelle's work published in this decade, we can seriously consider that inspiration for the Kingdom of Lira also came from this musical and poetic trend in Rio de Janeiro at that time. The necromantic undertones of Orpheus' tale and his use of the lyre would fit very well with the developing ideas about the *exus* and *pombagiras*.

The *exus* from the Kingdom of the Crossroads are usually called to open or close the ways for someone, to achieve victory over enemies, peace in trials, to teach sorcery and magic, bring health or disease, open locks and break chains, raise the poor from poverty and ruin the rich, for clairvoyance, to unite couples,

---

*de Janeiro na Primeira República*, Luiz Sergio Dias.

122 Brave.

123 Skilled.

124 Scumbag.

125 Rascal.

126 "The mythical cycle of Orpheus reaches an unusual vogue in Brazil from the 40s / 50s of the 20th century, motivated perhaps by the greater diffusion of the poets Fernando Pessoa and Rainer Maria Rilke between us." In *Perfis de Orfeu na poesia brasileira recente*, Antônio Donizeti Pires.

bring progress and backwardness, etc. After my own experience I can say that the Queen of the Seven Crossroads is a Master of Magic.

Before the creation of the kingdoms division of Quimbanda, the Exus of the Crossroads with their Exu-Rei were identified with the Line of Malei; up until the 1966 first edition of *Como Desmanchar Trabalhos de Quimbanda* – Volume I (*How to Undo Works of Quimbanda*) by Antônio Alves Teixeira Neto (Antônio de Alva) this was still the reference used, and in this work we are provided with a very interesting description of the Exus of the Crossroads:

The Spirits that work in this Line are the EXUS of crossroads and they have the aspect of the DEVIL from Catholicism. They present themselves with horns, have legs and hooves of a goat. Some present themselves in the form of monkeys, others under the figure of a bat. They have over the head a dull reddish light. They wield tridents and their bosses use swords. They cause the vices of drunkenness, gambling addiction, cause sexual impotence, being also specialists in matters related to the sexual functions, uniting and separating couples.

Any work thus is done at a crossroad in the shape of a cross and not in the shape of a "T"; this one is the crossroad of POMBA-GIRA; it is always under the care of these spirits; although others also act at the crossroads.

We see here that the rise of the kingdoms did not happen (or wasn't acknowledged) as late as 1966, that the Exu-Rei was still not matched with a queen and that Pombagira was still just the name for an entity (and not for a category) that ruled specifically at the "T" kind of crossroads.

The symbol of the Kingdom of the Crossroads is composed of two crossed tridents; the colors attributed to it are black and red; the day of the week Wednesday; the planet Mercury and the holy day the seventh of July.

## The Queen of Hearts

I bought my main image of the Queen of the Seven Crossroads during a trip to Rio de Janeiro in 2014. That was before my wife and I were initiated in what our mother-of-saint called "Chefatura de Quimbanda"[127] – a series of ceremonies during which the initiated lies for seven days in her House of Exus. I bought the image on a hunch (I was impressed with its beauty) and when I returned to the city in which we were living (Itacaré, in the state of Bahia) I asked my wife what she thought I had inside the package: *Dona Sete*, she answered after looking at the box for an instant. "Dona Sete" ("Lady Seven") is what the Queen of the Seven Crossroads is called affectionately in the southern states of Brazil where the Crossed Line of Umbanda developed.

Since then I began to work regularly with the Queen of the Seven Crossroads; besides the main image which I keep in a small shrine at home I have a smaller one that travels with me. Usually I make sessions of invocation at the altar every Friday at midnight. It was during one of these ceremonies of invocation that she asked me to write this small book about her.

---

127 There is not a proper way to translate "chefatura"; it comes from *chefe* (chief), indicating the role of command that entitles someone to work in Quimbanda. I do not know of a similar nomenclature in use in Brazil; this mother-of-saint used to say that she learned her practices in Bahia as much as in Cuba, and I suspect she mixed elements of different traditions in her brand of Quimbanda.

I had a similar experience before, when my wife's *pombagira*, Maria Padilha of the Souls, asked me to co-write a book about her with my wife.[128] During my work with the *Grimorium Verum* Chiefs, Astaroth asked me to put her sigil on the first pages of my *Thesaurus Magicus* III, and the Queen of the Seven Crossroads had asked for her *ponto riscado* to be on the cover of my *Scientia Diabolicam* anthology.

It was during these works and through some synchronicities that the Queen of the Seven Crossroads identified herself to me with the card of the Queen of Hearts (in Portuguese "Rainha de Copas", Queen of Cups). The identification of course is very apt as the *pombagiras* are usually associated with love magic; but when I researched the subject I found even more interesting connections.

Since the 15th century, identities were ascribed to the Court Cards in France, some taken from Greek Mythology and others from the Bible; it so happens that the Queen of Hearts card was attributed to the Biblical heroine Judith.

---

128 *Maria Padilha: Queen of the Souls*, Humberto Maggi & Verónica Rivas.

Image [Jeu de cartes au portrait officiel à une tête de 1816] :
[estampe] / Gatteaux, Nicolas-Marie (1751-18?)

Judith is the main character from the deuterocanonical book
named after her; it tells the story of a rich and virtuous Jewish
widow that uses her beauty and courage to seduce Holofernes,
the general of an invading army. Appearing before him, she used
her majestic appearance to impress him and utter false promises
and prophecies that very much pleased all those present.

Then her words pleased Holofernes and all his servants;
and they marvelled at her wisdom, and said,

Queen of the Seven Crossroads

There is not such a woman from one end of the earth to the other, both for beauty of face, and wisdom of words.[129]

Holofernes planned to get Judith drunk at a feast, "for he waited a time to deceive her, from the day that he had seen her",[130] but she outsmarted him and in the end he was left alone and passed out in his tent with her.

Then she came to the pillar of the bed, which was at Holofernes' head, and took down his fauchion from thence,
And approached to his bed, and took hold of the hair of his head, and said, Strengthen me, O Lord God of Israel, this day.
And she smote twice upon his neck with all her might, and she took away his head from him.
And tumbled his body down from the bed, and pulled down the canopy from the pillars; and anon after she went forth, and gave Holofernes his head to her maid;
And she put it in her bag of meat: so they twain went together according to their custom unto prayer: and when they passed the camp, they compassed the valley, and went up the mountain of Bethulia, and came to the gates thereof.[131]

I can understand why the Queen of the Seven Crossroads wished to identify her image with the heroine Judith: the Biblical tale is ripe with symbolism that enlarges and illuminates the powers and modes of actions of this *pombagira*.

---

129 Book of Judith 11:20-21. KJV
130 Book of Judith 12:16. KJV
131 Book of Judith 13:6-10. KJV.

Quimbanda and its predecessors were often identified as the magical weapon of the impoverished and oppressed, a way for them to get the upper hand against Church and State. The tale of Judith is a perfect example of how courage and cunning can be used to turn the tables and conquer a more powerful enemy, and because of that it became very popular during the Reformation, when the rebels had to face the might of the Catholic Church.

## Iconography

It is not known precisely when images for the *pombagiras* began to be produced and commercialized. An academic study on the iconography of Quimbanda located a surviving image that could be dated to approximately 1947.[132] Comparison between that image and a new version of the same entity revealed an interesting detail: the oldest image had *horns*; the newest was almost identical but the horns were removed.

That same study allows us to glimpse the world of the producers of images of Umbanda and Quimbanda, and the process through which the images come to life. In the creative process narratives and descriptions given by the entities themselves when incorporated, dreams and references to paintings, movies and even comic books all come together. A good part of the iconography was established in the 1970's and has suffered little change since then, but there is always space for innovation as the artisans in the small factories are open to new requests as much as the practitioners are open to receive new entities.

---

132 *Encruzilhadas da Cultura - Imagens de Exu e Pombajira*, Tadeu Mourão.

Carlo Francesco Nuvolone (1609–1662)
Judith with the Head of Holophernes.

Some characteristics of the images are very stable; of course, the Old Blacks and the *Caboclos* do not change the color of their skins; the *exus* and *pombagiras*, on the other hand, display more diversity: there are brown skin ("skin of exu", more typical) but also white skin ("skin of saint") and even the clearly diabolical red skin of some images. A picture from 1971 in Tadeu Mourão's book shows a very rare dark skinned *pombagira*, but I personally never saw one. The diabolical element, in fact, is the most characteristic, and is easily identified by anyone who sees an *exu* or *pombagira* image for the first time.

The erotic element is also strong in the *pombagiras*; most of the images are bare-breasted and have loose hair – immediately bringing to mind the descriptions of how the Portuguese witches used to operate.

The association between the representations of Pombajiras and the sorceresses narrows even more when we encounter the sculptural figuration of the Pombajira Queen of the Seven Crossroads. The emblematic smile that appears in most representations of the Pombajiras appears on the face of the nice queen, who, properly crowned and wearing a long red cloak, sits comfortably on her dark throne. At her neck is a symbol that again links Pombajira to the rituals of the Portuguese witches. A pendant that has a six-pointed star to the center hangs between the breasts of Seven Crossroads. Known as the Solomon sign, the hexagonal star was used in different rites, usually drawn on the ground, sometimes with salt.[133]

We have two traditional images for the Queen of the Seven Crossroads: standing and enthroned.

The standing image has the following items: crown, skull wand in the right hand, red cloak with golden details, a small sheathed sword on the left side of the waist, boots; the lower part of a red bikini has a belt with a golden cat face. The image is usually bare-breasted but some have the bust covered. Seven

---

133 *Encruzilhadas da Cultura - Imagens de Exu e Pombajira*, Tadeu Mourão.

QUEEN OF THE SEVEN CROSSROADS

crosses at the feet help to identify the entity, as the same model can be used for different *pombagiras*. Behind her there is a great yellowish fire. A hexagram hangs from a chain on the neck.

The crown of course is the main element which identifies her as a queen, but besides that it may also say she is a *crowned pombagira*, an entity that after being "baptized" to work for Umbanda progressed enough to decide to only do good deeds. The skull wand represents her power over lesser spirits of the dead: the skull in Umbanda and Quimbanda symbolism usually refers to the souls of the dead. This reminds us of the wand of Hermes, which is one of earliest models for every magical wand reputed to control spirits. In the image of the queen it combines the power of authority with magical power.

The small sword is full of possible symbolic meanings. From the same Homeric poem in which we find the Hermetic wand to control spirits we also have the oldest reference for the use of the sword to keep spirits at bay: Odysseus used a sword to prevent the souls of the dead from coming near the blood of the sacrifice. But the sword of the Queen of the Seven Crossroads most likely is there to remind *the living* of her power to kill them. It is one of the reasons her identification with the Biblical heroine Judith is very apt: the tale of Judith serves to warn us that, like the Queen of Hearts from the book *Alice's Adventures in Wonderland*, she may ask for someone's head. Some consider that Lewis Carroll was inspired by Elizabeth I of England to create the Queen of Hearts; more than 800 people were executed during her reign, including Mary, Queen of Scots, who was beheaded.

The cat face in the belt is also associated with European sorcery; when we come to the enthroned version, we find the cat again, in fact two of them, as sculptures on the arm rests; the Queen of the Seven Crossroads usually has her hands on their heads. She still wears the same outfit, the cat belt included, but on the throne she does not hold the skull wand and does not carry a sword. A new element here, still connected to European sorcery, is the green toad. Sorceries with black cats and toads abound in the Portuguese *Book of Saint Cyprian*, where we also find mentions of the Solomonic sign, the hexagram which also appears in the enthroned image. On the top of the throne it is common to see two or three skulls.

The enthroned image of the Queen of Seven Crossroads may have been inspired by one of John William Waterhouse's paintings, *Circe Offering the Cup to Ulysses*.[134] We know that *The Birth of Venus* by Botticelli was used to create a very popular image of one of the *pombagiras*, as the similarity is undeniable; although we cannot be so sure with the *Circe*, both images represent a sorcerer queen on a throne with feline images in the arm rests and a toad on the floor before the throne.

---

134 *Encruzilhadas da Cultura - Imagens de Exu e Pombajira*, Tadeu Mourão.

Circe Offering the Cup to Ulysses,
John William Waterhouse (1891).

# THE WORK OF SORCERY

———— ◆ ————

The essence of Quimbanda resides in the incorporation of the entities through the mediums in the *giras*. The spirits' words, spoken through the mediums, are the source of information for specific works done for specific situations – more so than traditional recipes.

The interchange is simple: mediums are paid in cash, spirits receive offerings and sacrifices. Here we have the true continuity with the African traditions as well as with European witchcraft practices, which in turn go as far back as Mediterranean Antiquity when Saint Cyprian worked his erotic spells for payment.

The reason for such kinds of sacrifices and offerings has been questioned at least as far back as Porphyry's challenge to the practices of the theurgists; the main argument usually revolving around the contrast between the material aspect of the offerings and the spiritual nature of the entities. Iamblichus in the 4th century and the Umbandists in the 20th attempted to explain that and the uses of other materials in their ceremonies. For instance, in Souza's pioneering work we find explanations like:

*Cachaça (sugarcane liquor)* – Because of its properties, it is a kind of disinfectant for certain fluids; stimulates others, the good ones; attracts, by aromatic vibrations, certain entities, and others drink it when incorporated, by virtue of reminiscence of material life.

*Tobacco* – It acts by the vibrations of the fire, and of the aroma. The smoke neutralizes the adverse magnetic fluids. It is often seen a person healed of a headache or relieved from the momentary discomfort of a sore, by a puff.

*Incenser* – It acts by the vibrations of the fire, and of the aroma, by the smoke and the movement. It attracts beneficient entities and repels the undesirable ones, exerting a pacifying influence on the organism.

I will leave the subject here with only one remark: no matter what the explanation is for the sacrifices and offerings, *the spirits ask for them.* If the practitioner is open-minded and sensitive enough to listen to the spirits, they will ask for these things and will reciprocate when they are done.

This having been said, I will add that I work differently from what is done in the *giras*. My personal experience with incorporation was always very weak and infrequent. I did my Chefatura of Quimbanda in December 2014 and it was an amazing and very important event in my life. However, my approach to the spirits was by then centered on altar work where the spirits manifest, communicate and commune with the practitioner.

The Queen of the Seven Crossroads is the spirit from Quimbanda with whom I have established the most lasting relationship. In fact, it started months before my Chefatura of Quimbanda, by which time I was writing my paper *The Gnosis of the Devil.* It was with her that I had one of the strongest ecstatic experiences during a ritual.

She asked me to write a book about her, and for months I did not have a clue how to do it, until the moment that it became clear and I started to find research material about Quimbanda that clarified a lot of blind spots I'd had and which allowed me to expand my view about this line of work.

During this period the Queen of the Seven Crossroads gave me a few hints about working with her that should be mentioned here. The offering of choice she gave to me is very simple: a black chicken roasted[135] with red onion. We should know that there

---

135 It should be very well roasted to the point of being crunchy.

are two ways to give this kind of offering: it can be left with other elements at a proper place, or it can be left for a time in front of the altar and afterwards consumed. To share a meal with deities was an important feat in Greek religion and we have examples of this in the Greek Magical Papyri.

This book is aimed more at the practitioner who wishes to contact and commune with the retinue of the Quimbanda spirits, especially with their Queen, without being part of a regular place where the *giras* with music and dance and possession occurs. The establishment of an altar allows for a different kind of experience, one that is more intimate.

After identifying herself with the myth of Judith, during one of my altar works with her on a Friday's midnight, she instructed me to rip a page of the Bible from the Book of Judith and add it as a small scroll at her altar; it was a doubly antinomian act for me as I highly value books and refrain from incorporating Christian elements in my practices (the Book of Judith is not part of the Torah and is even refused by some Protestant sects). Of course, as we saw, the Catholic element is also strong in Quimbanda and adding the prayer found on that page to my ritual in fact gave it extended meanings and an extra force. It is the blessing given to Judith after she brought the head of Holofernes to her city.

O daughter, blessed art thou of the most high God above all the women upon the earth; and blessed be the Lord God, which hath created the heavens and the earth, which hath directed thee to the cutting off of the head of the chief of our enemies. For this thy confidence shall not depart from the heart of men, which remember the power of God for ever.

And God turn these things to thee for a perpetual praise, to visit thee in good things because thou hast not spared thy life for the affliction of our nation, but hast revenged our ruin, walking a straight way before our God. And all the people said; So be it, so be it.[136]

Next she pointed me in the direction of the Seven of Hearts or Cups – something that in fact I should have thought of on my own. Crowley's Kabbalistic-Planetary interpretation of the 7's of the Minor Arcana is very negative, but looking at it with attention we can see it is very close to some of the key concepts we saw so far associated with Quimbanda in general and the *pombagiras* in particular:

The Seven of Cups is called Debauch. This is one of the worst ideas that one can have; its mode is poison, its goal madness. It represents the delusion of Delirium Tremens and drug addiction; it represents the sinking into the mire of false pleasure. There is something almost suicidal in this card. It is particularly bad because there is nothing whatever to balance it – no strong planet to hold it up. Venus goes after Venus, and Earth is churned into the scorpion morass. [...] This card refers to the Seven, Netzach, in the suit of Water. Here recurs the invariable weakness arising from lack of balance; also, the card is governed by Venus in Scorpio. Her dignity is not good in this Sign; one is reminded that Venus is the planet of Copper, "external splendour and internal corruption". The Lotuses have become poisonous, looking like tiger-lilies; and, instead of water, green slime issues from them and overflows, making the Sea a malarious morass. Venus redoubles the influence of the number Seven. The cups are iridescent, carrying out the same idea. They are arranged as two descending triangles interlaced above the lowest cup, which is very much larger than the rest.

---

136 Book of Judith 13:18-20.

This card is almost the "evil and averse" image of the Six; it is a wholesome reminder of the fatal ease with which a Sacrament may be profaned and prostituted. Lose direct touch with Kether, the Highest; diverge never so little from the delicate balance of the Middle Pillar; at once the holiest mysteries of Nature become the obscene and shameful secrets of a guilty conscience.[137]

A. E. Waite's take on the Seven of Cups is less drastic:

Strange chalices of vision, but the images are more especially those of the fantastic spirit. Divinatory Meanings: Fairy favours, images of reflection, sentiment, imagination, things seen in the glass of contemplation; some attainment in these degrees, but nothing permanent or substantial is suggested.[138]

When we use Tarot cards for practical magic, we must go beyond moral considerations and see them as talismans to work with specific kinds of energies; by pointing to the Seven of Cups the Queen of the Seven Crossroads shows the kind of energy and the types of magical works she identifies with. In the Rider-Waite tarot deck, for example, each cup gives a different insight into possible magical operations.

---

137 *The Book of Thoth: A Short Essay on the Tarot of the Egyptians*, Aleister Crowley.
138 *The Pictorial Key to the Tarot*, Arthur Edward Waite.

# Saravá Pomba Gira

We see that in the 70's the individuation of the *pombagiras* was already in place. N. A. Molina, a very prolific writer who published between 40 and 50 books all in this decade, dedicated a small volume to Maria Padilha[139] and in his work *Sarava Pomba Gira* he clarified that:

> At the beginning of this small volume, dedicated only to the Pomba Gira, Woman Exu, I want to clarify that we have many Pomba Giras, who from the moment they have a name, are considered baptized, each one of them having more seven unnamed, known as obsessors, as they are known in the Terreiros by the Sons of Faith.[140]

Molina dedicated his small book "with all my respect, affection and special attention to the Pomba Gira Queen of the 7 Crossroads, the companion of the dear Friend and Vigilante, Exu King of the 7 Crossroads". I have being wondering if the title of "queen" in the Quimbanda really came from Maria Padilha, as it is usually believed; another very strong possibility is that it came by extension from the title of the King of the Seven Crossroads, which would make the Queen of the Seven Crossroads the primary Queen of Quimbanda. To strength the argument, we see in the Portuguese and even in the Spanish spells that invoke Maria de Padilla or Maria Padilha a notable absence of any reference to her as "queen". The historical origins of the real Maria de Padilla apparently were forgotten in Brazil by the time the Quimbanda developed, which is clearly indicated by the fact that the majority of people believed her to be of French origin.

---

139 *Saravá Maria Padilha*, N. A. Molina. 1st edition published in 1973.
140 *Saravá Pomba Gira*, N. A. Molina. 1st edition published in 1973.

Testifying to the process of multiplication of the *pombagiras* that was in progress in the 1970's, Molina gave a list of "the best known names among us"; the Queen of the Seven Crossroads is the first and Maria Padilha is not mentioned:

Pomba Gira Queen of the Seven Crossroads
Pomba Gira Queen of the Cruzeiro
Pomba Gira of the Crossroad
Pomba Gira of the Fig Tree
Pomba Gira of the Calunga
Pomba Gira of the 7 Calungas
Pomba Gira of the Portress
Pomba Gira Maria Mulambo
Pomba Gira of the Sepulture
Pomba Gira of the 7 Shallow Sepultures
Pomba Gira Gipsy
Pomba Gira of the Cemetery
Pomba Gira of the Beach
Pomba Gira Girl
Pomba Gira of the Souls

According to Molina, we have an "incalculable number" of *pombagiras* but the one that has the title of Woman of 7 Exus is the Queen of the Seven Crossroads; these Seven Exus are "powerful chiefs of lines, divided each in 7 phalanges, and she acts as their woman". The Seven Exus according to him are:

Exu King of the Seven Crossroads
Exu Lock-Street (Tranca-Rua)
Exu Tiriri
Exu Marabo
Exu of the Mango Tree

Exu Veludo ("Velvet")
Exu of the Rivers

The Queen of the Seven Crossroads "always works together with the Exu King of the 7 Crossroads" and she is one of the few *pombagiras* who receive *despachos* ("dispatches"), offerings, etc., in crossroads in the shape of "X" (the others receive their works in the "T" crossroads), as well as in the Cruzeiro of the Cemetery. Molina subscribes to the concept that the identity of the Exu or Pombagira that is associated with a medium depends on the Orishas the medium has in his or her "head". The Exu of Oxalá for instance is given as the King of the Seven Crossroads himself – which again indicates the preeminence of the Crossroads, as Oxalá is the highest of the Orishas of Umbanda; the Queen of the 7 Crosssroads for Molina is "the negative representative of the line of Oxala" because for him the masculine is the positive pole of energy and the feminine the negative. In the Umbanda that Molina followed we see rescued the idea that "the Exu and the Pombagira are intermediaries between the man and the Orisha, working thus as a servant of the same, because they execute the superior orders when required by them".

Molina's book offers us three works to be done for the Queen of the Seven Crossroads:

## WORK OFFERED TO THE POMBA GIRA QUEEN OF THE 7 CROSSROADS

Buy in advance the following material: a clay pot, a white candle and a black and red candle, a bottle of anise, a cigarillo, a matchbox, a bottle opener, a pound of maize corn, a bottle of Palm oil, 7 open red roses (not rosebuds), a black and red towel, acquired the fabric according to the possessions of the Son of Faith.

On a Friday day, near midnight (*hora grande*, great hour), go to an X-shaped crossroads. Arriving there, first salute Ogun right in the center of the Crossroads, because as you may already know, the center of the Crossroads belongs to Ogum, the Warrior Orisha; therefore, to him is made a treat. In this place, light the white candle, in his honor.

At the end of this part, we ask for his protection, walking then 7 steps backwards, choosing soon after one of the corners of the crossroads, where the despacho is made for Pomba Gira, proceeding as follows: first, stretch the black and red towel in the chosen place, then place in the center the clay pot, with the corn meal and the Palm oil already mixed, so that it is in the form of a pulp, then opens the bottle of anise, pouring it as a little cross out of the towel, saluting the Pomba Gira Queen of the 7 Crossroads, placing, after this task, the bottle next to the bowl, then light the black and red candle by placing it on the outside of the towel, thus avoiding that it burn the towel when it finishes burning, soon after light the cigarillo, placing it on top of the matchbox, after giving six puffs up.

Finish by arranging the 7 red roses around the offering, in the form of a horseshoe. Finally, offer the despacho saying the following: Queen of the 7 Crossroads, I offer you this gift, asking for your protection, your help, and that you always work my way; then ask for leave, taking 7 steps backwards, and then thanking Ogun before retiring, since he is the Orixá who supervises the Crossroads, it is the Orixá that determines all the works in the Crossroads, therefore he is asked for leave, both when arriving as when leaving the crossroad.

## GREAT WORK OFFERED TO POMBA GIRA QUEEN OF SEVEN CROSSROADS AS FIRMNESS

In advance the Son of Faith must acquire the material to be used, thus avoiding embarrassments and last-minute setbacks.

The material is as follows: a black and red towel, about one meter in size, and the fabric can be purchased according to the possessions of each one, when the towel is made it must be the same size in the red part as in black, skirting the same with hem or fringe in red color. I said that each one can use the fabric according to the possessions of each one, but do not forget that the Queen of the Crossroads is a little demanding, and likes a good treat, always receiving the best; because giving of the good and the best, she will not forget to give back to the requests made, this because the one who gives always receives.

Buy a clay pot, cornmeal, a bottle of palm oil, 7 good quality cigarillos, 7 boxes of matches, seven candles all red, 21 red and open roses (do not use rosebuds, only roses already open) , seven bottles of anise or cocktail of cachaça, fruit and sugar, seven white cups that have never been used (virgin). With the material already acquired, minutes before going to the street prepare, picking up the clay pot, put the maize corn and mix with the palm oil, thus forming a yellow farofa, so called by us. This part being ready, on Friday near midnight, known as the great hour and also called the open hour, go to an "X" shaped crossroads, and there arriving, right in the center of the same salute Ogum; because as everyone should know, he is the absolute owner of the center of the Crossroads, he is he Orisha who supervises and completely dominates the Crossroads, where all the people of Exu is used as servants, for this reason is that Ogum is called King of Sorcerers.

Continuing, after saluting the owner, right in the middle of the Crossroads, ask him for permission to lower a despacho, retreat back seven steps going to one of the corners of the Crossroads because this is the exact location that belongs to Exu and Pomba Gira, and in this place, lower it as follows: first stretch the black and red towel, then in the center of it put the clay pot, which should already be with the farofa made from cornmeal and oil palm, then light the red candles, one by one, placing them around the towel, in the outside, thus avoiding that they burn the towel, then open the bottles of aniz by pouring a little crosswise out of the towel, saluting Pomba Gira Queen of the 7 Crossroads, and then fill one of the cups by placing it next to the bottle on top of the towel, proceeding with the remaining 6 bottles and cups, forming a circle around the bowl, then lighting the cigarillos one at a time , giving three puffs to the top, placing a cigarette on top of the matchbox, which must remain open with 7 sticks pulled out, and always facing the center of the despacho, doing the same with the remaining 6 cigarillos, after decorating around with the 21 red roses and the despacho should be arranged as follows: the towel stretched with the candles lit on the outside, the clay bowl in the center, and around in a circle, arrange the bottles of anise, each with the respective cup full beside it followed by a matchbox with the cigarillo lit on it, circling around with the red roses.

At the end of this drop, the Son of Faith will say the following: Queen of the 7 Crossroads, accept this gift from this offerer, and I ask you for strength, firmness, light, and great protection. Finishing, ask license to leave and take 7 steps back, not forgetting to thank also Ogum, for his help and protection, also asking him for leave to withdraw.

Very important remark: This despacho, in the form of an offering, or of treat, must be made on a Friday at midnight, and the offerer can take the pot with the farofa already prepared, or if you wish, you can even make the mixture on top of the Crossroads, at the time of the drop, because I think it will be received with greater pleasure and firmness.

The cups can be replaced by glasses, and they should never have been used before, filling all seven with aniz, each with its bottle and arranged in a circle.

The candles when they are bought, in this type of despacho, must be all red, not black and red, for, as you know, red represents the force, the vibration; with black and red the sense is quite different; represent the force, the War, the demand, the darkness, the tenebrosity. Therefore, whenever we give as a gift, we offer the red candle, asking for light and strength.

Do not forget to ask Orisha Ogun in the center of Crossroads, both when arriving and leaving, thanking this wonderful orisha. As for the place to lower despachos for Exu and Pomba Gira, one should only make the drop in one of the four corners of the Crossroads.

The Son of Faith, in making the towel, may do according to his possessions and will do it in black and red color in equal parts, and may adorn the outline with a red fringe.

Saravá Queen of the 7 Crossroads.

## WORK OFFERED TO POMBA GIRA QUEEN OF THE 7 CROSSROADS WITH THE INTENTION TO DEMAND HARM TO THE ENEMY PERSON

On a Friday, go to a crossroads in the form of "X", called male crossroads. Arriving, right in the center, salute Ogun and then ask him license to drop a despacho for Pomba Gira Queen of the 7 Crossroads. After that is done, in one of the corners of the crossroads light a black and red candle, in homage to the Pomba Gira Queen of the 7 Crossroads, after do the same in 5 more crossroads so that you already passed 6. When you reach the 7th and last Crossroads, in one of the corners stretch a black and red towel, open a bottle of marafo,[141] pouring a little in a cross shape, saluting Pomba Gira Queen of the 7 Crossroads.

Then place the opened bottle in the center of the towel and next light 7 cigarillos, giving with each one three puffs to the top, placing them on the boxes of matches that should, all of them, be ajar with the cigarillo on top, tidy up in the form of horseshoes or a circle around the bottle. Finishing, light the last black and red candle, placing it on the side of the towel. Finishing this part, make the request saying the following: Queen of the 7 Crossroads I ask you to take care of so-and-so (say the complete name of the enemy person), and make the request according to the desire and need of each one, finish giving 7 steps back, and then thank Ogun, at the crossroads center, and leave.

The material must be purchased in advance and as follows: 7 black and red candles, a bottle of sugarcane liquor and the black and red towel.

---

141 The *marafo*, also called *marafa* (corruption of *malafa*), is a sugarcane liquor especially prepared for religious uses.

Note: Do not forget that for 6 consecutive crossroads in one of the 4 corners light one of the black and red candles, and that the total drop will only be done at the seventh crossroads.

The crossroads should be all in sequence, without interruption, otherwise, this type of work will not have the value desired by the offerer.

Do not forget that the Queen of the 7 Crossroads is the Pomba Gira wife of the King of the 7 Crossroads and that in a work of demand he will act jointly with his wife. Therefore, this Pomba Gira has the value, in short, of an extraordinary force in her works.

I want to draw the attention of the Son of Faith that when finishing the drop of this despacho, you should not in any way turn back to look, and at the end, when you are at the 7th and last crossroads, do not go back at all by the same way, because if so, the work will be broken, that is, it will have no value.

Saravá Pomba Gira Queen of the 7 Crossroads.

Saravá the King of the 7 Crossroads.

## Ponto Riscado

It is very difficult to find images of the *ponto riscado* of the Queen of the Seven Crossroads in these old books; Molina himself, who gave so much prominence to the Queen, provided 15 *pontos riscados* of *pombagiras* but did not explicitly give her name to any of them. From the list of 15 other known names he gives in the beginning of the book, he provided *pontos riscados* clearly identifiable for only 6, with 4 of them receiving 2.

Pomba Gira of the Calunga (2)
Pomba Gira Maria Mulambo (2)
Pomba Gira Gipsy (2)
Pomba Gira of the Beach (1)
Pomba Gira Girl (2)
Pomba Gira of the Souls (1)

Then we have 2 *pontos riscados* apparently of a general use; we cannot be sure, however, that mistakes were not made and the correct name of the *pombagiras* were not inserted properly:

PONTO DE EXU POMBA GIRA   PONTO DE EXU POMBA GIRA

The first *ponto riscado* in the book belongs to a "Pomba Gira of the Cruzeiro", a Pomba Gira not in the list that may be in fact the "Pomba Gira Queen of the Cruzeiro".

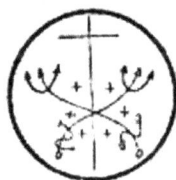

PONTO DE POMBA GIRA DO CRUZEIRO

Then we have the *ponto riscado* of the "Pomba Gira Queen"; as there is not one single mention in the book of a *pombagira* with that name, we can consider that this is in fact the *ponto riscado* of the Pomba Gira Queen of the Seven Crossroads:

The usual format of the *pontos riscados* is inside a circle; some quimbandeiros believe it is done like that to keep the power of the *exus* and *pombagiras* under control. I received myself so far three *pontos riscados*, one for Maria Padilha Queen of the Souls,[142] one for the Queen of the Seven Crossroads (below) and the third for the Queen of the Cemetery (page 135); all lack the circle:

I received only a few brief explanations for this one; that it is a Key and that the two serpents on the upper part are connected to Lucifer's power. In fact, the Queen of the Seven Crossroads said that this *ponto riscado* is "to exalt the power of Lucifer". When I received it I experienced how powerfully the energy can manifest through it.

---

142 *Maria de Padilla: Queen of the Souls*, Humberto Maggi and Verónica Rivas.

In the same session she also connected the Queen of Clubs[143] with the Pomba Gira Queen of the Cemetery, and gave me the *ponto riscado* below; the inverted pentagram is drawn in black and the candle is red. She is devoted to works of Black Magic and her special place is the Cruzeiro.

Image[Jeu de cartes au portrait officiel à une tête de 1816] : [estampe] / Gatteaux, Nicolas-Marie (1751-18/0

---

143 The name of the Queen of Clubs in the French system is "Argine", an anagram of Latin "regina" (queen). In the French decks she is the only one of the Four Queens that holds a flower in one of her hands. Her identity was never properly explained.

That the entities themselves are the source, or a source, for the *pontos riscados* is easily seen at the *giras*, when the possessed mediums often draw the designs with the *pembas* on the floor; what we have in the literature of Umbanda and Quimbanda is just a very small fraction, with many *pontos riscados* being drawn just once for specific works and never registered.

The "pontos riscado are emblems elaborated by the Exus to identify themselves when they incorporate in their children, mainly in the sessions of Umbanda. Usually, the Exus dash the point and light candles on them to build a center of strength for performing magical operations.[144]

Souza also left an earlier explanation for this:

**Ponto Riscado** – It is an emblematic or symbolic drawing. It attracts, with the concentration that determines it to be traced, the entities or phalanges to which it refers. It always has a meaning and sometimes it expresses many things, in few strokes.

Even more interesting, Souza's work contains a narrative that, although being gruesome and hard to believe, gives us a very good insight into the concept of the magical power of the *pontos riscados*:

To prove the strength of the magical points (emblematic, cabalistic or symbolic designs), he [the medium possessed by an Exu] produced a sensational demonstration. He selected seven people, ordered them to concentrate without breaking the chain of thought, drew a ponto

---

144 *Exu do Brasil: tropos de uma identidade afro-brasileira nos trópicos*, Vagner Gonçalves da Silva.

[riscado] on the ground, and beheaded a cat whose body he ordered to be removed, leaving its head next to the ponto.

– As long as that ponto is not erased, that cat does not die and that head does not stop meowing.

"For seventeen minutes, the severed head of the body was painfully miaowing in the room, while outside, the headless body struggled with life. The assistants were beginning to be terrified. He erased the ponto, and ceased the groaning meowing of the bodiless head and the convulsions of the headless body.

## Ponto Cantado

The *pontos cantados* combine the percussion music from the African rituals with the versified invocations from Portugal and Spain. They describe key features of the entities they invoke and the kind of works they perform. Again, let's turn to Souza's book for an earlier interpretation of this:

> **Ponto Cantado** – It is often an incoherent hymn, because the spirits who teach us, compose it so as to achieve certain effects on the material plane without revealing aspects of the spiritual plane. It has, thus, a double meaning. It acts by the vibrations, it operates fluid movements and, harmonizing the fluids, it helps the incorporation. It calls some entities and moves others away.

We have a few important things mentioned here: that the *pontos cantados* are composed and transmitted by the spirits (through the possessed mediums) and that they have "fluidic" and "vibrational" effects that both invoke and banish spirits. We see here how the vocabulary of the Umbanda and Quimbanda owed to the pseudo-scientific ideas from Kardecism. This kind of explanation was extended to almost every aspect of the ritual, like the use, for instance, of the small dagger probably added to the repertoire of Umbanda after influences from European magic:

*Ponteiro (Pointer)* – It is a small dagger, preferably with crosshead on the handle. It serves to calculate the degree of efficiency of the works, because the contrary fluidic forces, when they have not been broken, prevent it from nailing or they bring it down, once it has been fixed. It also has the influence of steel, in relation to magnetism and electricity.[145]

I selected two of the oldest *pontos cantados* of the Queen of the Seven Crossroads from one of Molinas's books from 1975:[146]

| Pomba Gira Rainha das Sete Encruzilhadas | Pomba Gira Queen of the Seven Crossroads |
|---|---|
| Eu sou Rainha nos Sete Encruzo | I'm Queen in the Seven Crossroads |
| Em cada um tenho morada | In each one I have an abode |
| Eu quero filho pra defender | I want son to defend |
| E inimigo pra espetar | And enemy to spear |

---

145 Souza, Leal de. *O Espiritismo, A Magia E As Sete Linhas De Umbanda*. Editora do Conhecimento; Edição: 2ª. 2008.

146 *3777 Pontos Cantados e Riscados na Umbanda e na Quimbanda*, N. A. Molina.

## Pomba Gira Rainha da Encruzilhada

Ela é mulher de Sete Exu
Ela é Pomba Gira Rainha
Ela é Rainha da
Encruzilhada
Ela é Mulher de Sete Exu

\*

Eu moro lá na encruzilhada
No meu encruzo eu sou uma
Rainha
É lá que faço e quebro
demanda

\*

Me chamo Pomba Gira
Rainha eu sou
É na minha encruzilhada
Onde tenho minha morada
Eu sei trabalhar, eu sei
trabalhar

É, é, é na Umbanda
Vem, vem, vem
da Quimbanda
É Pomba Gira que
vai girar, vai girar

## Pomba Gira Queen of the Crossroads

She is the wife of Seven Exu
She is Pomba Gira Queen
She is Queen of the
Crossroads
She is Woman of Seven Exu

\*

I live there at the crossroads
In my crossroads I am a
Queen
That's where I do and I break
demand

\*

My name is Pomba Gira.
Queen I am
It's at my crossroads.
Where I have my home
I know how to work, I know how
to work.

Yes, it is, it's in Umbanda
Come, come, come from
Quimbanda
It's Pomba Gira that's going
to spin, it's going to spin.

| | |
|---|---|
| É na banda do mar | It's in the band of the sea |
| E´,é,é, na | It is, it is, it is in the |
| Umbanda | Umbanda |
| Vem, vem da | Come, come from |
| Quimbanda | Quimbanda |
| Pomba Gira vem trabalhar | Pomba Gira comes to work |
| E levar o mal para as | And bring the evil to the |
| ondas do mar | waves of the sea. |
| | |
| Pomba Gira chegou | Pomba Gira arrived |
| Pomba Gira girou | Pomba Gira spun |
| É a mulher dos | She is the woman of the |
| Sete Exus | Seven Exus |
| Sa Pomba Gira chegou | Lady Pomba Gira arrived |

\*  \*

| | |
|---|---|
| Eu sou a Pomba Gira | I'm the Pomba Gira |
| E estou sempre presente | And I'm always present |
| Sem mim não existe festa | Without me there is no party |
| Quem confirma é minha gente | Who confirms is my people |
| Estou sempre nas festanças | I'm always in the parties |
| Brincando com alguém | Playing with someone |
| Estou sempre nas festanças | I'm always in the party |
| Eu saravo minha rainha | I salute my queen |
| E o meu rei também | And my king also |

\*  \*

| | |
|---|---|
| Tataretá, tataretá | Tataretá, Tataretá |
| Pomba Gira vai chegar | Pomba Gira will arrive |
| Pomba Gira chegou | Pomba Gira arrived |
| É a mulher de | She is the woman of |
| Sete Exus | Seven Exus |
| Sa Pomba Gira chegou | Lady Pomba Gira arrived |

QUEEN OF THE SEVEN CROSSROADS

Author's personal altar.

# APPENDIX

## Tables of Influence

| Greek Witches | Latin Witches | Judeo-Christian |
|---|---|---|
| Circe | Mesopotamian | Eve |
| | Witches | Witch of Endor |
| **Medea** | | **Lilith** |
| | Erichto | Queen of Sheba |
| Simaetha | Canidia | **Herodias** |
| | Pantha | **Maria Magdalene** |
| ⬇ | Sagana | |
| | Meroe | |
| Morgana | Pamphile | ⬇ |
| ⬇ | Photis | |
| | Folia | Inquisitorial Witch |
| **Maria de Padilla** | Proselenos | |
| | Oenothea | ⬇ |
| | Dipsas | |
| | | |
| | ⬇ | Prosecuted Witches |
| | | (exiled to Brazil) |
| | **Witch of Évora** | |

In Table 1 the names highlighted in **bold** refer to persons or characters who received at some stage some kind of cult of worship. Herodias, the princess of the Herodian dynasty of Judaea who asked for the head of John the Baptist through the seductive dance of her daughter, was believed during the Middle Ages to be the supernatural leader of a cult of witches.

| Exu | Feminine Orishas | Bantu Ancestors |
|---|---|---|
| Orishá Exu | Nana | Pai Quibombo |
| | Iansa | *(as an example)* |
| Bombojira | Oxum | |
| | Yemanja | |

# Bibliography

Apollonius, and R. L. Hunter. *Argonautica*. Cambridge University Press. 2015.

Apostolica, Paenitentiaria. *Enchiridion of Indulgences: Norms and Grants*. Catholic Book Publishing. 1969.

Asante, Molefi Kete., et al. *Encyclopedia of African Religion*. SAGE. 2009.

Assis, Antonio de. *Dicionario Kimbundu-português: linguístico, botânico, histórico e corográfico*. Santos.

Azevedo, Janaina. *Orixás Na Umbanda*. Universo Dos Livros. 2010.

Bethencourt, Francisco. *O imaginário Da Magia: Feiticeiras, Adivinhos e Curandeiros Em Portugal No século XVI*. Companhia Das Letras. 2004.

Bouche, Pierre. *Sept Ans En Afrique Occidentale: La Côte Des Esclaves Et Le Dahomey*. E. Plon, Nourrit. 1885.

Capone, Stefania. *A Busca Da África No candomblé: tradição e Poder No Brasil*. Pallas. 2018.

Chatelain, Heli. *Folk-Tales of Angola. Fifty Tales, with Ki-Mbundu Text, Literal English Translation, Introduction, and Notes*. 1894.

Clay, Jenny Strauss. "The Hecate of the Theogony". *Greek, Roman, and Byzantine Studies*, Vol 25, No 1. 1984.

Costa, Valéria Gomes, and Gomes Flávio dos Santos. *Religiões Negras No Brasil: Da escravidão à pós-emancipação*. Selo Negro Edições. 2016.

Crowley, Aleister, and Frieda Harris. *The Book of Thoth: A Short Essay on the Tarot of the Egyptians*, Being the Equinox, Volume III, No. 5. Weiser Books. 2008.

Edmonds, J. m. (translator). *The Greek Bucolic Poets*. 1923.

Ellis, A. B. *The Yoruba-Speaking Peoples of the Slave Coast of West Africa, Etc.* (Photomechanic Reprint of the Edition of 1894.). Anthropological Publications. 1966.

Fontenelle, Aluizio. *A Umbanda através Dos séculos*. Edição Da Organisação Simões, 1953.

—. *Exu*. Editôra Espiritualista.

—. *O Espiritismo No Conceito Das religiões e a Lei De Umbanda: Venerável Ordem Espiritualista iniciática Universal*, Templo de Alá. 3a edição. Editôra Espiritualista.

Geoffrey, and John Jay Parry. *The Vita Merlini*. University of Illinois. 1925.

Griffiths, Emma. *Medea*. Routledge. 2006.

Hawthorne, Walter. *From Africa to Brazil: Culture, Identity, and an Atlantic Slave Trade*, 1600- 1830. Cambridge University Press. 2010.

Hebert, Jill M. *Morgan Le Fay, Shapeshifter*. Palgrave Macmillan, 2013.

Hesiod, and Homer. *The Homeric Hymns and Homerica, with an English Translation*. Harvard University Press, 1936.

Homer, and A. T. Murray. *The Odyssey, with an English Translation*. W. Heinemann, 1938.

Homer, et al. *The Iliad*. Harvard University Press, 1924.

Jones, Lindsay, and Mircea Eliade. *Encyclopedia of Religion*. Macmillan Reference USA, Thomson Gale. 2005.

Lele Óchani. *Sacrificial Ceremonies of Santería: a Complete Guide to the Rituals and Practices*. Destiny Books. 2012.

Lopes, Nei. *Enciclopédia Brasileira Da diáspora Africana*. Selo Negro Edições. 2011.

Maggi, Humberto, and Verónica Rivas. *Maria de Padilla: Queen of the Souls*. Hadean Press. 2015.

Marques, Rodrigo. *Os outsiders do além: um estudo sobre a quimbanda e outras 'feitiçarias' afro- gaúchas*, Leistner. URI: http://www.repositorio. jesuita.org.br/handle/UNISINOS/4314

Molina, N. A. *3777 Pontos Cantados e Riscados Na Umbanda e Na Quimbanda*. Editora Espiritualista, 1976.

---. *Saravá Maria Padilha*. Editora Espiritualista. 1973.

Mourão, Tadeu. *Encruzilhadas Da Cultura: Imagens De Exu e Pombajira*. Aeroplano Editora, 2012.

Petropoulos, J. C. B. *Greek Magic: Ancient, Medieval and Modern*. Routledge. 2013.

Ramos, Arthur. *O Negro Brasileiro*. Ministério Da Cultura, Fundação Biblioteca Nacional. 2001.

Rio, João do. *As Religiões No Rio*. 1951.

Ronan, Stephen. *The Goddess Hekate*. Chthonios, 1992.

Silva, Vagner Gonçalves da. *Caminhos Da Alma: memória Afro-Brasileira*. Selo Negro. 2002.

Verger, Pierre. *Notas Sobre o Culto Aos orixás e Voduns Na Bahia De Todos Os Santos, No Brasil, e Na Antiga Costa Dos Escravos, Na África*. EDUSP. 2000.

Waite, Arthur Edward. *Pictorial Key to the Tarot, in Full Color*. Causeway Books. 1973.

Queen of the Seven Crossroads